THE MAIN CURRENTS OF MARATHA HISTORY

THE MAIN CURRENTS OF MARATHA HISTORY

GOVIND SAKHARAM SARDESAI

GYAN

Published by

Gyan Publishing House
5, Ansari Road
Daryaganj, New Delhi-110002
Phone: 011-47034999, 9811692060
E-mail: books@gyanbooks.com

Distribution Network
gyanbooks.com
India, USA, Canada, UK, Australia

ISBN: 978-93-7316-290-4 (PB)

First Published, 1933

2nd Impression 2025

Printed at: Gyan Press, Delhi.

THE MAIN CURRENTS OF MARATHA HISTORY
Author: GOVIND SAKHARAM SARDESAI

THE MAIN CURRENTS

of

MARATHA HISTORY

Originally Patna University Readership Lectures 1926,
now greatly enlarged, rewritten, and brought up to date.

BY

GOVIND SAKHARAM SARDESAI, B.A.

EDITOR, *Selections from the Peshwas' Daftar, Poona.*
AUTHOR OF *Marathi Riyasat, Handbook to the Records in the Alienation Office, &c.*

1933

" Man is as he has made himself,

Man will be as he will make himself."

" It is evident that there is no quality upon which the success of a nation so much depends as upon its courage. No nation can rise to a high place without being brave. It cannot maintain its independence even; it cannot push forward upon any path of life without courage. Nations that are cowards must fail."

D. G. E. Hall—

The Soul of the People,"—*Macmillan.*

PREFACE

[1933]

Since the first edition of these lectures was printed seven years ago, a great advance has taken place in the research of Maratha history, particularly on account of the ample selections from the *Peshwas' Daftar* published by the Government of Bombay. While editing these selections I had to wade, with the help of my staff, through the vast mass of old papers, both historical and administrative, and naturally obtained an insight into many useful topics, which I consider indeed to be more valuable than the papers actually published. I do not like to allow this experience to perish with me and am ardently seeking means to put it on record. In the mean time the demand for copies of my Patna Lectures has long been pressing, and I am now trying to meet it immediately after obtaining relief from my undertaking at the *Peshwas' Daftar*. While revising these lectures for a fresh edition, many new points have struck me for which I have now tried to make room without materially altering either the original plan or the size of the book. The main object of these lectures was to interpret Maratha history from purely Maratha standpoint, to those who cannot study the original materials at first hand owing to their ignorance of the language. This object I have scrupulously followed even now. But there were obvious gaps in the performance when it was first executed. No mention was made about the rise and career of Shivaji, or the grand successes of Peshwa Bajirao I. and his brother. A sudden jump was taken from the death of Shahu to the Maratha War with the English, thus skipping entirely over the important event of Panipat or the brilliant career of Madhaorao I. These topics I have now put in and incidentally made a few alterations in my discussion of the character and achievements of Mahadji

Sindia and Nana Phadnis and of the causes of the Maratha downfall which form the subject of the last chapter.

My readers will bear in mind that I have by no means attempted to write herein a full history of the Marathas. My purpose is to supply a running constructive criticism and a reasoned interpretation of the salient features involved in that vast subject, more or less following the lines of Sir Alfred Lyall, in his brilliant work, *The British Dominion in India,* although I do not claim to possess his critical powers or his sound judgment. Having purposely avoided entering into minute details and thereby making the treatment cumbrous, I have tried to explain the aims and objects, the strong and weak points, the motives and general nature of the Maratha power, correcting and adding what appeared necessary from a personal study and experience, and removing the misconceptions and wrong views which I happened to notice during the course of my reading. Readers may judge how far I have succeeded in this rather ambitious design. All I can claim is that the views herein expressed are entirely my own, as any presentation of historical topics is bound to be. It would be absurd in an undertaking of this kind to try to please this or that school of thought. But I know I have tried to avoid partisanship and to give out an impartial reading of the Maratha days. If history is to be of any practical use, an unbiassed and fearless criticism is, in my opinion, most essential, and, in this respect, I feel I have tried to meet the educational needs of all students so far as the Maratha period of Indian history is concerned.

I cordially repeat what I wrote in the first edition, viz. that, ' the Patna University have laid me under deep obligations, by undertaking to have the lectures printed promptly and under my personal supervision at Calcutta. I cannot also omit to thank my valued friend Prof. Sarkar for the kind and ready help he has rendered me in this task, shewing thereby what a keen interest he takes in Maratha History.'

Kamshet,
Dist. Poona
1st Dec. 1933

G. S. SARDESAI

CONTENTS

Lecture I

MAHARASTRA DHARMA,—THE IDEAL OF THE MARATHAS

Lecture II

HISTORICAL RESEARCH IN MAHARASTRA

Lecture III

SHIVAJI'S CONCEPTION OF A HINDU EMPIRE

LECTURE IV

SHAHU AND THE MARATHA EXPANSION

LECTURE V

DEVELOPMENT OF MUSLIM-MARATHA CONTEST

LECTURE VI

MAHADJI SINDIA AND NANA PHADNIS

LECTURE VII

THE DOWNFALL OF THE MARATHA STATE

THE MAIN CURRENTS

of

MARATHA HISTORY

LECTURE I

MAHARASTRA DHARMA THE IDEAL OF THE MARATHAS

1. *Muslim influence did not penetrate into the south.*

The one subject of great historical importance on which many eminent scholars in Maharastra have concentrated their attention in their research, has reference to the prime aim of the Marathas, I mean, the conception of their swarajya, their object in striving for it, the principles for which they stood, the main unifying force which heartened them in times of trouble and adversity, and enabled them to work for national uplift for some two hundred years. The subject is obviously vast and intricate, and ranges over a large extent of literature, tradition, and the lines of succession of very many saints, teachers and leaders of the Maratha people. It would be very instructive to examine it from old writings and records, and from the mass of literature produced by many recent scholars, who have thought and written on the subject. I cannot, therefore, do better than take it up for discussion, at the beginning of my task, by way of clearing the ground of Maratha history in general, and present to you a few facts and views and some of the important results of study and research in Maharastra on this basic subject. It was that great scholar and thinker M. G. Ranade who, in his brilliant work *The Rise of the Maratha Power*, first described the process of nation-building in the Deccan, and set down *Maharastra Dharma*, the duty of Maharastra, to be its guiding principle. The original and full meaning of this phrase requires a searching examination, so as to furnish for us the clue, by which we can understand, why of all the nationalities of India, the Marathas alone found it possible to establish an independent power for a pretty long time.

India south of the Narmada was never completely subjugated by the Muhammadans, in the sense in which northern India was. The Hindu princes in the north, from the time of Jaipal and Prithviraj to that of Rana Sanga had struggled hard but in vain to roll back the onrushing tide of Muslim conquest. The Rajput princes were entirely crushed ; they became servants of the Emperors, contracted marriage alliances with them, and submitted to them in all matters of religion and discipline. The sacred places of the Hindus were violated, their temples were pulled down, their religious practices were interfered with ; in other places, wholesale populations were converted to the Muslim faith. One has only to visit any important city in northern India, in order to realize the havoc caused to Hindu temples, images, palaces and to old Sanskrit inscriptions, as, for instance, at Dhar and Mandugad, in fact, to all that every nation cherishes as sacred and inspiring. An old *bakhar* of Mahikavati (Mahim near Bombay), finished in 1578 by one Bhagawan Nanda Dutta, with many portions written centuries before that time, has been discovered and printed. It contains the following description of the terribly depressing condition of north Konkan, after it fell into the hands of the Muhammadans in 1348. Says the author : " All religion was destroyed ; ties of friendship and relationship vanished ; the Kshatriyas lost all sense of duty towards the country. They gave up their arms and took up the plough instead. Some took up the profession of mere clerks and the rest were reduced to the humiliating position of slaves and Shudras, while a host of others were wiped out of existence. Most of the people lost their self-respect and the Maharastra Dharma was totally destroyed." But, while the Hindu mind in the north had helplessly submitted to violence and force, the onward march of Muslim conquest received a strong check in the south, where the invasions of Alauddin Khilji and Malik Kafur had but made a transitory impression. The fierce hand of Muhammad Tughlak could not win the Deccan for Delhi, and although the rebellious Hasan Bahmani established an independent dynasty at Gulbarga, that kingdom, for all practical purposes, was a Hindu rule with only a nominal mixture of the Muslim element.

For two hundred years preceding the birth of Shivaji, forces were at work in the Deccan, facilitating Hindu independence at different centres of more or less magnitude and influence. Shivaji only supplied the adhesive element unifying the scattered units, and shrewdly worked upon the religious sentiment, which so strongly appealed to the popular imagination. Rajwade aptly differentiates this spirit of Maharastra from that of the other provinces of India, by calling the former *jayishnu* or "conquering", and the latter *sahishnu* or "passively suffering." This genius or spirit of Maharastra runs unmistakably through the utterances of her saints and preachers, and through the actions of her warriors and diplomats. The expression *Maharastra Dharma* is known to have been used for the first time by the author of a popular Marathi work *Guru-Charitra* or 'the life of the great Guru Dattatreya'. composed somewhere about the middle of the 15th century, although the Maratha saints had preached and spoken of Maharastra Dharma long before. The late Prof. Limaye, a great authority on history, says : "What the saints of Maharastra did was to create the moral force that would exalt and ennoble the political ideal of the Marathas. There were two main factors making up this national movement, the one representing the political power wielded by the more or less independent Jagirdars or Deshmukhs (of whom I am going to speak in a later discourse), who opposed Shivaji in his early career, and the other represented the moral force, which the people derived from the preaching of Ramdas and other great saints. Shivaji stands forth for the synthesis of the two. Himself the son of a great Maratha nobleman and as such possessed of power and influence, he was thoroughly imbued with the spirit of the teachings of the saints. Inspired by their high ideals, he strove to realize them in his life and in doing so, he was prepared to risk both his power and position. That is the significance of Shivaji's life-work, and it is that which entitles him to rank by the side of the greatest of the world's heroes".

2. *The two traditions of Devagiri and Vijayanagar blended in Shivaji.*

At the outset we must remember that Shivaji did not start his national work all of a sudden. His three predecessors in the family were all clever men, imbued with the national spirit common to all Marathas, in an increasing degree in succession. They all seem to have been clearly inspired by the traditions coming down to them in two distinct currents, the one starting from the Yadavas of Devagiri of the 13th century on the northern border of Maharastra, and the other from the *Rays* of Vijayanagar of the 16th century on the southern; the first coming through Shivaji's mother Jijabai, who was descended directly from the Yadavas, and the other from his father Shahji, whose life-work was cast in the historic regions of Vijayanagar. The grand titles assumed by the Yadava kings such as Pratap Chakravarti, Samasta-Bhuvanashraya, Samrat, Shri-Prithvi-Vallabha, and their national banner bearing the golden image of an eagle * were vivid emblems fresh in the Maratha memory, directly inspiring them with ancient glory, liberty and independence. Similarly as regards the *Rays of Vijayanagar*, the famous Deva-Ray concentrated his attention on improving horsemanship as the principal arm of guerilla warfare, particularly suited to the hilly broken country of the Deccan, which Malik Ambar and Shahji successfully employed in resisting Mughal aggression and which later on Shivaji and his successors so cleverly developed and so successfully utilized in attaining their life's purpose. An old paper records a dialogue between Rama Ray, the victim of Talikot, and his mother, when,

---

* सुवर्णगरुडध्वज.

on the eve of the famous battle (January 1565), he went to beg her blessings for his success. Says Rama Ray : " This our country has been a favourite resort of our gods, Brahmans, religion, and charities. Five Muhammadan kings have combined and conspired to destroy it. In order to prevent such a catastrophe, let me, mother, go with all my forces and conquer them. Do you confer your blessings on me." This conversation describes the attitude of the Hindu mind and shows how the spirit of religion had inspired it to rise against Muhammadan oppression in the south long before Shivaji, who simply took up the cue later with the same object, as the *bakhars* and other records go to prove. The influence of the teachings of the saints and particularly of Ramdas, I will have occasion to explain later, and need not repeat it here.

The tradition from Vijayanagar acted differently. It fostered young Shivaji's rebellious spirit. He did not relish the part his father had played in the service of Bijapur. "God did not relish" says the chronicle of the Peshwas prepared by Nana Phadnis in 1783, " the wicked part Shahji had taken in helping the Turks to convert India into a Muslim land and put down the Hindu faith. " Shahji accompanied the Bijapuri general Randaula Khan during 1637-39 for the conquest of Western Karnatak. Govinda Vaidya the author of Kanthirayanarasa-Charitam thus describes the atrocities perpetrated in this expedition. " Randaula Khan and Shahji marched against Virabhadra Nayak of Ikkeri and laid siege to it. They were armed with guns, rockets and slings. They placed terrific guns on the bastions. The Turks took possession of the fort, captured women, smote off the heads of marble images of gods, plundered the temples and the town, insulted the honour of virtuous ladies and slaughtered cows. Having joyfully taken possession of the articles in the palace, Randaula Khan posted guards on the town and returned shortly after to the Court of the Padshah, presenting the spoils to him. " This explains the growth of Shivaji's revolt.

The famous verse adopted by Shivaji and ever since continued by his successors as an inscription on their

State seal, is another strong evidence of the same spirit. It runs thus :—"Ever-growing like the crescent of the first moon, and commanding obedience from the world, this seal of Shivaji, the son of Shahji, shines forth for the good of the world."* The late Mr. Bhave, a penetrating scholar, maintained that this verse was formerly used by the Moreys of Javli on their seal ; Shivaji borrowed it from them, making a few suitable modifications of his own.

3. *How Maharastra Dharma or the Maratha spirit actuated the Marathas up to the last.*

This vein of Maharastra Dharma not only sustained the nation through their most terrible trials during their long struggle with Aurangzeb, but was faithfully kept up through the subsequent transformations and later expansion of the Maratha empire. The first four Peshwas have left ample evidence of their having ever kept this ideal of Maharastra Dharma before their eyes. In all their undertakings in the north, and their dealings with the Rajputs and other races, they steadily strove, not so much for empire or power, as for the release of the famous holy places of the Hindus from the Muhammadan hands, *viz.*, Prayag, Benares, Mathura, Hardwar, Kurukshetra, Pushkar, Gadamukteshvar and others ; in the end they succeeded in taking possession of nearly all, except Prayag and Benares, which never came back into Hindu possession. In a memorable letter which Shahu addressed to his cousin Sambhaji, when the latter leagued with the Nizam, Shahu says : "This kingdom belongs to gods and Brahmans : the blessings of god Shankara and goddess Bhavani enabled our great and revered ancestor Shivaji to rescue it from the hands of the Muhammadans. What a pity it is, then, that you should have given up our Maharastra Dharma and sought shelter with the enemies of it. Our family boasts of descent from Ramdevrao Yadava ; it does not therefore behove you to go contrary

---

* प्रतिपच्चंद्ररेखेव वर्धिष्णुर्विश्ववंदिता ।
शाहसूनोः शिवस्यैषा मुद्रा भद्राय राजते ॥

to our grain."* Shahu's greatest Peshwa Balaji Bajirao was so fully imbued with this spirit of religious liberty for the Hindus, that, in a letter of 1752 he asks his agent residing at the Court of the Nizam to remind him (the Nizam) that, "We Maratha *ganims* are the disciples of the great Shivaji Maharaj", conveying thereby a hint as to how they were actuated by religious motives in their dealings with the various potentates of India, and how they were trying to complete what Shivaji had undertaken.

Even as late as the early nineties of the 18th century, the famous Maratha diplomat Govindrao Kale, who long resided at the Court of Haidarabad, thus writes to Nana Phadnis, and congratulates the Maratha Government on the signal achievements of Mahadji Sindia in regulating the affairs of the Emperor at Delhi, and fulfilling the objects of Maratha policy. The letters and despatches of this Govindrao Kale have been printed in several volumes, and show him to have been a man of high principles and great capacity, fully breathing the Maratha atmosphere of those days. I shall quote the letter in full, in order to give you a correct idea of what the Marathas of those days felt and talked about : "If I were to adequately express what I have felt, upon reading your most inspiring letter, giving an account of the crowning glories achieved by Mahadji at Delhi, I should have to write volumes ; still I cannot repress my enthusiasm, and I make myself so bold as to transgress the ordinary limit, and write some of the uppermost thoughts of my mind. Each single item gives occasion for a separate congratulation. India extends from the Indus to the southern ocean ; beyond the Indus comes Turkistan ; these limits of India have been under Hindu control since the days of the Mahabharata. But some of the later Hindu kings lost their old vigour, and yielded to the Yavanas who therefore became powerful. Delhi was captured by the Chagtais ; the culminating point came in the reign of the great Emperor Alamgir. Every sacred thread was subjected to a tax of Rs. 3/8

---

* See Life of Shahu by Chitnis, page 54-56

for payment of jazia : *pucca* or cooked food came to be offered for sale in shops, and people were compelled to buy it. This oppression brought about a reaction. The epoch-making Shivaji rose in a small corner to protect the Hindu religion. Thereupon came such luminaries as Peshwa Balajirao and Bhau Saheb, who gave fresh light and hope to the whole of India. This spirit later on possessed Mahadji Sindia so much, that he was able to fulfil the ancestral purpose. If we had *tawarikh*-writers like the Muhammadans, they would have written volumes on Mahadji's victories, for they know how to magnify small things up to the skies. We Hindus are of a reverse temperament. We do not speak out even about signal doings. Impossibilities have indeed been achieved. The Patil-bova (Mahadji) broke the heads of those who tried to raise them. All wished him ill luck, but he did accomplish his object dauntlessly. This victory will surely bear the desired fruit on the model of the great Shivaji. Let no evil eye soil this glorious result. Not only have territories and kingdoms been acquired by this victory, but the protection of the Vedas and the Shastras, the foundation of religion and unmolested worship, the preservation of Brahmans and cows : in fact, this suzerain regal power of the Marathas, this fame and glory, all have now been achieved and proclaimed in the loudest accents to the world. To preserve this grandeur will be the glory of Patil-bova and yourself. You must not be remiss in this task. All doubts about our supremacy over India have been set at rest. Grand Maratha armies must now be stationed on the plains of Lahore, for there exist countless evil-doers, who rejoice at our reverses and try to compass our downfall." Poor Govindrao did not conceive of a new danger from the west through the sea !

I have purposely quoted this long letter which is dated 2nd July 1792, that is, exactly ten years before the transfer of the sovereign power from the Maratha hands into the British. Many letters of Nana Phadnis are extant addressed to Mahadji Sindia urging him to obtain from the Emperor a transfer of the Hindu holy places from Muhammadan control and an explicit circular order prohibiting the slaughter of cows throughout India. Such an order was obtained and paraded with great pomp in Poona. I need not stress this point further, having made it sufficiently clear, not only how the great ideals were constantly surging in Maratha minds right up to the last, but how high their spirits were, even when their fall was imminent, as we now know.

4. *Meaning of Maharastra Dharma*

I am not here discussing how far this ideal of Maharastra Dharma was right or whether it was harmful, and whether in the long run it did good or evil to India as a whole. This point I shall have to discuss later. I only wish to emphasize that history has been missed by very many writers, owing to their inability to grasp and trace this Maratha ideal through the character and action of the race as well as their literature and history, like the ancient Hellenic culture, which is said to have actuated the Greeks in their national expansion. The best minds in Maharastra have devoted their energies to the discussion of this topic ever since the days of Ranade, and have time and again, proved by fresh evidence the existence of this grand purpose, of which I have not been able to present here more than a bare outline. Materials discovered in Maharastra have been read and discussed so frequently and so exhaustively, that I could not very well omit this pervading topic in my talks on Maratha history. *Radha-Madhava-Vilasa-Champu*, *Mahikavati-Bakhar*, *Shiva-Bharat*, *Parnala-parvata-Grahan-Akhyan*, *Talikot-Bakhar*, the *Shakavalis*, the *Rajaniti* of Ramchandra Amatya, and the letters and papers of Shahji and his ancestors, and the utterances of older bards and saints, as also inscriptions and documents about gifts to temples and Brahmans during Maratha and pre-Maratha times, all these are growing in volume and importance every day, and testify to the existence of this religious spirit of Maharastra Dharma in the minds of the people for a long time. Shahji was the patron of poets and literature ; two of his proteges,

Jayaram and Paramanand, wrote several works, which have recently been discovered and printed and deserve careful study.

Says Rajwade : "Those born in Maharastra are called Mahárástrás=Marástra, corrupted into Maráthá. The country inhabited by the Maharastrikas came to be called Mahárástra. All the Hindu castes from the Brahmans to the *Antyajas* residing in that country, obtained the comprehensive name Marástra or Maráthá. The religion of these Marathas came to be called by a comprehensive title Maharastra Dharma. It includes four elements *viz.*, (1) practices towards gods and injunctions of the Shastras (*Deva-Shastrachara*) ,(2) local practices (*Deshachara*) (3) family practices (*Kulachara*) *and* (4) caste practices (*Jatyachara*). The inhabitants of Maharastra were bound to follow all these." Says Justice Ranade : "The only motive power which is strong enough to move the masses in this country is an appeal to their religious faith. During the last 300 years the whole of India had been visibly moved by the new contact with the Muhammadan militant creed, and there had been action and reaction of a very marked kind, particularly in Maharastra." I cannot enter into the details of this problem here, which requires patient and original study, and which is difficult to grasp merely from translations. But to understand Maratha history properly, all the sources must be read in the original and considered in their proper light.

5. *Evil effects of this Maratha ideal*

Let me say frankly that however useful this ideal of Maharastra Dharma might have been in securing national interests in the beginning, to me it appears as not an altogether healthy one. Its main drawback was that it made the Maratha mind entirely inert and unprogressive. Dominion means progress, and unless there is provision for making changes to suit the changing requirements of succeeding times, no power can last long. This spiritual ideal of the Marathas was often unpractical, giving rise to a rule in practice, amounting to " we must not change the old, must not take up the new." Shahu acted on this principle for 40 years and made it the condition of his transfer of power into the hands of the Peshwas at the time of his death. Even now we painfully realize how tenaciously the Indian mind sticks to old unpractical Shastras and their injunctions, as in the case of the removal of untouchability, even though they had been proved unsuitable to our present situation. In all practical matters of the Hindus, every item of life is based on religion. We are proud of quoting, in season and out of season, the Smritis and the Shastras in support of what we may happen to be doing. This conservative turn of mind prevented the Marathas from acquiring new education and new ideas, from travelling to western countries, or training their own men in science and western warfare, so as to introduce new methods and processes of work into their constitution. How this affected the Maratha power I shall relate later on. For the present it is enough for me to point out, how the failure to detect this underlying and unifying principle of Maharastra Dharma, has led many a writer to describe Maratha rule as mere outbursts of an inborn tendency for ravaging, pillaging, destroying and doing good to nobody. This wrong notion has much vitiated the character of Maratha history and requires correction.

6. *Visible marks of Maratha influence along the sacred rivers*

It is interesting to trace the results of Maratha rule to this ideal of Maharastra Dharma and examine them from the general character of the people. We look in vain for a Taj Mahal or a Qutb Minar in the works left behind by the Marathas. We know, of course, they never had the leisure, the peace and the money that are necessary for such constructions. But even if they had these, they never in my opinion possessed the requisite inclination. The Maratha race, as their soil and history have made them, are a rugged, strong and sturdy people, intelligent, self-assertive and practical, having in their mental cast the urge of utility towards life and action, patient, industrious and penetrating in learning and study, hardy, frugal and calculating in their temperament, but not emotional or showy idealists. They always had an eye for practical interests and the conveniences of life, in all that they planned and accomplished. Whatever one could expect from such a character and from their religious turn of mind already alluded to, has doubtless been profusely in evidence in the Deccan and elsewhere, Wherever Maratha influence penetrated they built temples, bathing ghats on rivers, tanks and wells, walls and forts, residential palaces contrived for protection and convenience, serais and hill-passes. The temples and their vicinities were usually the places for schools where the Vedas and the Shastras were taught, their cost being defrayed from assignments of land or cash, styled *anna-chhatras*.

The Maratha edifices are by no means pretentious. They are ingenious in conception and exquisite in execution, when minutely examined. Big black stones were specially brought to the Deccan from the river Gandaki for working them into images, some of which are indeed remarkable for their skill and art. Most of these temples and images are to be found in out-of-the-way places, away from the railway, and have hardly attracted the notice of the present day advertising travellers. About 30 years ago the late Rao Bahadur Sane, a touring Maratha official in the Educational Service, had occasion to visit nearly every village in the Poona and the Kolaba Districts of the Bombay Presidency, and being fond of observation, kept a record in the form of a diary, in which he wrote down every peculiar point that met his eye. Extracts from these diaries, which have recently been published,* yield a most valuable and interesting account of the relics of old Maratha rule and conclusively prove that, after all, that rule was not so barren of results as is generally supposed. Water-works, temples, tanks,

*_Vividha-Dnana-Vistar_, Feb. 1915 to August 1920.

images, palaces and forts are to be found nearly everywhere built by the various Sardars and Jagirdars who served in distant parts of India, but who had a sort of a home capital in the Deccan. Jambgaum of the Sindias, Wafgaum and Chandwad of the Holkars, Davdi and Nimbgaum of the Gaikwads, are only a few among the plentiful existing types of the past Maratha constructions. The old Peshwas' palace at Nasik, now occupied by the District Judicial Courts, is indeed a monument worth being called a work of art. The tank at the shrine of Jejuri on the top of a hill is large and beautiful, having been constructed by Bajirao II. The paths of the ghats and the temples there, are all well executed and exhibit care and skill of construction. The temple of Bhuleswar in the same vicinity is also a fine building. The Katraj tank, which then supplied water to the city of Poona, was executed by Peshwa Baji Rao II. The temples and images at Pandharpur, Theur, Chinchwad, Alandi and Gangapur are indeed excellent specimens of the works which the Peshwas executed. The skill and proportion of the stone images will indeed beggar description. The ghat on the Bhima at Pimpalner, the small but beautiful tomb of Mastani at Pabal, the temple of Someswar at Chas, the temple and tank at Karanjgaum and Verul, the temple of Lakshmi-Nrisinha at Narsingpur built by Vithal Shivdev, the temple and travellers' houses at Morgaum, the Vishnu Mandir at Uran, constructed by the Bivalkars,—these and various others of this type, will, if properly brought to public notice, certainly prove that the Marathas were not entirely devoid of artistic skill, or a sense of beauty; nor was their rule so barren of results as many in ignorance have supposed.

But mere grandeur, waste and lavishness, were not in their grain; temples, rivers, conveniences of water and residence, hill-paths and ghats, spacious and convenient dwellings, designed more for use and protection than show, have received every attention from the Maratha rulers, who cannot therefore be charged with the neglect of works of real public utility. This tendency of Maratha constructions is also amply visible in northern India, wherever the Maratha influence penetrated. It requires examination and study. The fact is, that under the general impression that the Marathas were merely vandals and freebooters, few have cared to investigate and bring to light those unpretentious, but impressive and often exquisite relics executed during the Maratha times. The cursory exploration of only two districts mentioned above, ought to be extended to the other districts and distant corners of Maharashtra, and all available papers, objects and traces of historical interest brought to light for the use of students and scholars. I can say from personal experience, that heaps of papers and material of great utility are still to be found in all important centres of Maratha activity, awaiting the search and sympathetic handling of earnest workers and well-to-do publishers, who care for our historical past. The Rastes of Wai, the Patwardhans of Miraj and Sangli, the Pratinidhis of Aundh and Karhad, the Surves of Shringarpur, the Shirkes, the Jadhavs, the Moreys, the Jedhes, the Nimbalkars and Ghorpades had all had their centres of work and influence, small capitals, so to say, of these historical families, wherein they concentrated all their attention, money and labours for over 200 years.

The grand and rich valleys of the two sacred rivers, the Godavari and the Krishna, with their numerous tributaries offer a most fruitful field, not only for search and collection, but for the publication of useful illustrated guides or albums, based on a national historical conception. The Godavari starts from Trimbak, a place in mountain fastnesses to which the Peshwas and the leading families paid frequent visits of pilgrimage ; a few miles below are two places hallowed by the residence of two historical female figures, Anandvalli, the residence of Anandi-Bai, wife of the famous Raghoba, and Gangapur the residence of Gopika-Bai, wife of Peshwa Balajirao and mother of three brilliant but unfortunate sons of historical fame : Viswas Rao the eldest lost his life at Panipat ; his younger brother Madhav Rao died a premature death from consumption at the age of 28, after a splendid rule of 11 years, full of grand achievements ; and the third and youngest, Narayan Rao, was murdered at the instigation of his uncle Raghoba. Their mother Gopika-Bai is said to have been so overcome by grief at this last bereavement, that she left her palatial residence at Gangapur in agony, and lived in a hut at Panchavati opposite Nasik, subsisting on the alms which she begged from door to door. Down the river stand Nasik and Panchavati, already too well known to need special mention. Sangvi, Kopergaum and Kacheswar, still lower down, are places abounding in relics of the latter day Peshwas. Puntambe, Nawase, Kaygaum and Toke, Shevgaum, Paithan, Rakshasbhuvan, Shahgad, Pathri, Nanded, Brahmeshvar and very many other places down this great river will, I am sure repay a thorough inspection and publication of illustrated old historical relics. As a race we lack that spirit of travel and observation which is to be found in the west, and which has yielded there such abundant results and topics of national interest.

The river Krishna, rising at Mahabaleshwar, offers a still more fruitful field for research and active interest. Dhom, Menavali, Wai, Mahuli, Karhad, Sangli, Miraj, Kurundwad, Wadi and other places lower down, all deserve to be investigated by means of an active campaign. I have not the time here to refer to smaller streams like the Bhima, the Nira and others, nor to the larger and more extensive valleys of the Tapti, the Narmada and the Chambal. The genius of the Maratha race has worked along river streams and among mountain fastnesses, which deserve to be thoroughly ransacked, if we wish to build up our historical past on authentic data. A similar research is also required outside Maharashtra in northern and southern India, particularly where the Maratha influence penetrated. Dhar, Dewas, Indore, Ujjain, Jhansi, Saugor, Gwalior, Banda, Mathura, Bithur, Benares, Nagpur and other places, not to mention many similar ones in the south, all bear plentiful signs of the influence and culture imparted by the Marathas, which will repay the labours of a special study. I have dilated on this point, specially to draw the attention of students to the various directions in which research can be and has yet to be carried on.*

In Maharastra such a campaign of research was started first by Rajwade and continued by a band of poor but devoted workers, whose tours and experiences have been printed in the annals of the *B. I. S. Mandal* of Poona, containing detailed descriptions of historical places, old monuments, folklore, village songs, obscure poems of old writers and bards, and other relics of bygone days. In the midst of our every day busy life, our students hardly command the leisure and the patience which such a careful study requires. Signs, however, are decidedly hopeful for historical research, when one notices at the present moment several earnest workers in distant parts of India busily engaged in sifting available sources and constructing a true story out of them.

7. *Influence of this political ideal on Marathi literature and society.*

So far at any rate as present research goes in Maharastra, the Marathas can rightly boast of possessing in a printed form, *Bakhars* or chronicles, personal and public letters, news reports, accounts, Government, documents, sanads and decisions, treaties, genealogies, diaries and chronological entries, and various other forms of historical material, which probably no other people of India has, in the same proportion or of the same variety. They are also different in nature from those of the other parts of India. Of all these papers, the letters are by far the most important in a historical sense, since, plentiful as they are, we can prepare with their help a connected account of all important events occurring in Maratha history and, nearly always, from different points of view. Since language is only the outward expression of the actual life and occupation of a people, Marathi literature

* An effort in this direction is being made during recent years by various organizations whose object is to foster fellow-feeling among the Maratha communities residing in outlying places styled Greater Maharastra, and thereby to increase the output of useful information bearing on various topics of our literature and history.

increased with the spread of their activities, from the time when Shivaji raised it to the status of the language of the Court, in the place of Persian. Important affairs of the army, navy, forts, justice, revenue accounts and other subjects, came all to be written in Marathi since Shivaji's days, and this change in a short time enriched that language to an enormous extent. With the increase of work many individuals and families coming from out of the way places, received fresh inspiration and encouragement.

There was hardly any prose worth the name in Marathi before the days of Shivaji, when all the best literature used to be in poetry and that too of a devotional and religious character. But when Shivaji and his father started their new work, battles, campaigns, treaties, engagements and orders constituted the engrossing activity of the day, and these required to be committed to writing. The adventures and achievements of Shivaji and his followers, his victory over Afzal Khan, for instance, or his visit to the Court of Aurangzeb, or the thrilling capture of Sinhagad by Tanaji Malusre, soon captivated the people's imagination, and Shivaji's mother Jijabai herself took the lead in getting them immortalized in bardic poetry for popular recitation all over the country. Samples of such songs, or *powadas* as they are popularly known, have been translated into English verse by Acworth, and will give to non-Marathi readers some idea of the activities of those days. Shivaji employed learned pandits to coin an official vocabulary by translating technical terms from Persian into Sanskrit and prepared what is called the Raj-Vyavahar-Kosh, *i.e.*, a dictionary of technical names for the use of the Court. The Persian element soon began to give place to Sanskrit, which came to be drawn upon for all kinds of high-flown writing, so that in a hundred years' time the character of the language was entirely changed. While Eknath, the greatest Marathi writer of the 16th century, uses nearly 75% Persian words and expressions in his works, Moropant's Marathi of the 18th century is nearly all Sanskrit with hardly a 5% mixture of Persian words.

There is a prevalent notion that modern Indian prose is a creation of the 19th century or the British days, started in imitation of the great prose writers of the west. So far as Marathi is concerned this notion is not quite accurate. A particular kind of prose writing of a very high order did come into existence during the 150 years of Maratha activity. Language, like industries and other national concerns, needs official patronage for its growth and prosperity, and when Marathi received the required patronage it shone all the brighter, as we can see for ourselves from the published papers. It is necessary for all of us to realize, in how many different ways Swarajya improves the status of a nation, and why all the world is striving for it. If a nation's soul is reflected in its literature, we can clearly read it in the prose chronicles of the Marathas, some of which will take a high rank among prose writings. Sabhasad's account of Shivaji, the *Bakhar* of Bhau Saheb, the *Kaifiyat* of the Holkars, and the two *Bakhars* of the Peshwas, are all compositions of a high class and correctly reflect the doings of the Marathas, their hopes and aspirations, their joys and sorrows, their capacities and short-comings. But it is the letters which would appeal to the reader most. They are written by experts with the particular object of impressing the writer's views upon the men in power, who were in charge of the executive government. More than a hundred printed volumes of such letters exist at present, which show how the writers (*Chitnises*) and translaters (*Parasnises*), came to be in great demand all over the country. Every Maratha leader had to employ expert writers in his camp, in order to despatch news, or explain a distant situation to the central authorities, and obtain definite orders on important and delicate affairs of State.

The members of the Chitnis family were all consummate writers, whole accumulated heaps of written matter strike the imagination wonderfully. When news-letters were received from distant places and read at Satara or Poona, some of the writers were at once noticed for their excellent style and cleverness, and were picked out for higher posts. Thus, as the empire extended, the art of writing received a great impetus. Some of the letters and documents of those days which we now read, possess indeed a very high literary character and show how cleverly the Marathi language and penmanship were cultivated. I have now and then given by way of samples English translations of some such papers in these discourses.* If a comparative estimate of these Marathi writings is made, I think, several of them will indeed take a very high rank and compare favourably with some of the best specimens of the diplomatic despatches of the west. I imagine the other nationalities in India have similar papers of historical value in their possession, and if they have not, they must try and make sure that they are not lying in oblivion, either in private possession or in State archives. Amatya Ramchandra Nilkantha, Khando Ballal and his son Govind Khando, Chimaji Appa and his son Sadashiv Rao, the Peshwas Bajirao and Balaji Bajirao and Madhav Rao, Brahmendra Swami, Shripat Rao Pratinidhi, Trimbakrao Pethe, the Purandares, the Hingnes, the Patwardhans, Nana Phadnis, his agent Sadashiv Dinkar, Krishna Rao and Govind Rao Kale, these and others, too many to be mentioned, were all capable and skilful writers, who have fully depicted in their productions the Maratha spirit of those days, making us feel as if we were living in those stirring times.

In the wake of the military leaders, great numbers of traders, merchants, accountants, bankers, engineers, and other craftsmen had to accompany Maratha expeditions for supplying the needs of war, colonization and administration, and showed great efficiency in executing their tasks. There were, besides, news-writers to convey information of the military and diplomatic operations at every stage, from one corner of the country to another. Revenue collectors and accountants kept records, and brought in tributes and other dues. Builders and engineers erected forts and battlements, and built roads, ghats and temples

*The author's *New History of the Marathas* recently published reproduces many papers of this nature.

on hills and river banks. Judicial and police arrangements followed in the wake of conquest, thus starting regular peaceful life for all workers in the country. Scholars, pandits, priests and saints soon followed when settled conditions were effected and, by means of personal character and devotion to duty, moulded the life of the outside people so as to make Maratha influence distinctly affect society and religion. They built temples, opened schools and free kitchens, and subtly and unobtrusively introduced for a time Maratha culture into the north, the inhabitants of which for a long time afterwards found this Maratha penetration healthy and beneficial. People in those days could perform their pilgrimages and return home, full of enthusiasm for the re-establishment of Hindu-rule throughout the land. They looked upon the Maratha leaders as the liberators and defenders of their faith.* The records of the Patankars at Benares, of the Hingnes at Delhi, of the Khers at Saugor, of the Kolhatkars in Nagpur and West Bengal, and of persons of lesser note at Lucknow, Mathura and Prayag, bear ample testimony to these side activities of the Marathas. No jarring note is to be detected in these peaceful efforts ; on the contrary the northerners appreciated them whole-heartedly. Any one who takes the trouble of studying minutely the contemporary accounts narrated in the old papers, and compares them in detail with the earlier Muhammadan invasions, during the Pathan period particularly, can easily realize the contrast between the two, and see how the penetration of the former was mild and congenial, and that of the latter destructive.

8. *Legitimate Maratha pride in past achievements.*

The Marathas alone of all the various nationalities of India, put forth the strongest organized opposition to the growing Mughal power, and ultimately crushed it. In the course of this process, they evinced capacity, tena-

* For cultural contact between the south and the north see the author's *New History of the Marathas*, vol. II chapter II section 2 and chapter X section 4 (social contact).

city, patience, and judgment, so that they can be very well called benefactors of India. They worked, in their own way and according to the standards of those times, for the welfare of the country, as much as was then possible for any Indian power to do. And if they had not been unexpectedly called upon to face an organized Western power, they would in all probability have created a Hindu empire in India. If, on the contrary, the Peshwas had not taken the supreme charge of the Maratha Government after the death of Shahu, the situation in the Deccan would at once have paved the way for British intervention in Western India, simultaneously with Plassey and Wandewash, which gave the British their first supremacy in Bengal and Madras respectively. The least credit, therefore, that must go to the Marathas, is that they put off the onrush of British arms into Western India by at least half a century. Otherwise, the Plassey of 1757 would have simultaneously seen its counterpart in the Deccan, resulting in a similar fate for Western India. A people that put down the Muslim power, that for long resisted the British advance in all parts of India, that conquered and civilized the Gonds and other tribes in the distant north and the south, that have left plentiful permanent marks of their influence in a quadrangular tract, of which the four corners may roughly be put down as Nagpur, Surat, Goa and Tanjore, that ever stood for order, peace and culture, and finally that saved the soul of India and inspired it with a new hope, are, in my opinion, entitled to a legitimate pride in their past history.

LECTURE II

HISTORICAL RESEARCH IN MAHARASTRA

1. *Extent, scope and limitation of historical research.*

A study of history means search for truth ; and truth is never one-sided. It would not be possible for the Marathas to write a complete history from their own Marathi papers only. At most they will show only one side of the picture. The other sides are imbedded in various other languages and, since Maratha history is but a part of the history of all India, however much it may appeal to Maratha sentiment, it must be completed from sources outside Marathi. A purely historical mind should be as impartial and analytical as a chemist's is in treating a piece of charcoal or diamond. A historian ought to possess the same impartial and critical attitude of mind in judging complicated human affairs, in order to sift truth from untruth, if his history is to prove serviceable. When, for instance, we have to treat of an event, say, the battle of Panipat, it would not do for us to rest satisfied with the Maratha records only. We must look for all possible light from whatever channel it may be available. In the first place, we have not got together even all the letters and accounts that the various Maratha Sardars and writers must have despatched from their places in that momentous campaign. But they had, in addition, dealings with the Rajputs, the Jats, the Emperor, his ministers, the various Rohilla chiefs, the Nawab Wazir of Oudh, the Sikh leaders and generals, besides the foreign traders (British, French and Portuguese). Their accounts and papers are to be found in their respective languages. In order, therefore, that we may obtain a complete picture of Panipat, we must try to secure all the foreign sources and then compose an account from them.

Even then the picture may not be perfect, for the human mind is always liable to err. If we see a fracas in the street happening before our own eyes, and if we have to give evidence about it in a court of law, we know how often each one has a different version to give, for each one observes only a part and that too from his own point of view. In this respect the human mind, which alone is the medium of communication, is like a piece of coloured glass ; as a ray passing through the colour, gets a tinge of it, so does the human mind get a tinge of the communicating medium. You can, therefore, realize how very difficult this process of forming historical judgments and conclusions is. Are we then to consider all history false ? No ; certainly not. Treat history in the spirit of a science and one would find it serviceable at every stage. Herein also lies the real value of history. If there be no difference in views, no variations in the estimates of men and events as set down by different writers, history will contain only stereotyped sets or bundles of facts unchanged and unchangeable. They would cease to be human or progressive, would give no exercise to the thinking powers of students, and prove more or less like scriptures to be taken on an authority never to be questioned. History deals with the civilization of man all round, which is ever changing and which at every moment affects the destiny of man. History must exercise the thinking powers of students, if they would treat the subject scientifically. If they do not take the trouble to arrange, sift and classify facts on their own initiative, do not wait to find out for themselves how far their own reason would be prepared to accept or dispute the correctness of those facts, it would no longer be a science. In history we must accept nothing on credence and authority, however eminent the authors may be.

2. *Indian history has yet to be constructed by a synthesis of materials from all sources.*

We can thus see how research is to be undertaken and what its limitations are. So far as Indian history is concerned, we are yet practically at the initial stage. European history, say that of England, France or ancient Rome and Greece, has long passed through these stages at the hands of many master minds, who have sifted the materials and given them a shape, which now can be accepted as more or less settled. A new fact may even now come to light here and there, and may change a little detail of this or that incident. But the main subject has been exhaustively treated. Besides the free nations of Europe are creating history every day ; in India, we have been hardly making any history at all, since the middle of the 19th century. We are passive on-lookers, struggling to obtain or create conditions and surroundings, which would enable us to make our own history. That is why the history of India since our downfall before the conquering power of Britain, ceases to interest us, ceases to fire our imagination, sentiment or pride. For instance, routed though the Marathas were on the field of Panipat, they yet take such a lively interest in all the incidents, persons or features of that memorable event, that their poets, research scholars, bards, actors, novelists are every day exercising their powers in writing about it ardently. The Shivaji-Afzal Khan incident or the murder of the Peshwa Narayan Rao equally fascinates and engages the Maratha mind. It is but human, that the doings of our ancestors or of the sages and heroes of our religion, should appeal to our imagination.

History, however, has to take account of all these, not from a sectarian point of view, but with a fixed purpose synthetically to mould one single complete national history of India, out of all those elements, that may have a concern with the period with which we are dealing. And since, we have to build up such a united national history of India, we need more and more materials for our study, as we reach our own more complicated times. In the earlier centuries we used to live a more isolated, exclusive and perhaps quiet life ; but in later times, with the increasing struggle for conquest and power, Indian affairs, whether political or social, became increasingly intermixed; particularly is this the case with the history of the 18th century, when, with the decline of the Mughal rule, the scramble for power and supremacy became more acute and involved more competitors. We can thus easily conclude what various sources of material we must look for, and in what directions we have to search for fresh light, before we can arrive at a fairly acceptable estimate of any given event. We have only recently been awakened to this part of our duty, and vigorous efforts in this field of national work are now being made by various scholars and bodies in the country. Steady and serious work always brings in a rich harvest. You can easily imagine how the life story of Shivaji, for instance, would have always remained incomplete and one-sided, had not Prof. Jadunath Sarkar brought to bear upon it his great powers of scholarship and investigation, when fortuitously he undertook the study of Aurangzeb, who had spent almost half of his long and active life in the midst of the Marathas. Sarkar's contribution to Maratha history is indeed invaluable, particularly as regards the materials available not only in Persian but in several European languages, which he has been able to secure after tremendous labour, expense, and patience, and which he has ably shown how to utilize in constructing a synthetic history of India as a whole. Various other gentlemen are now seen to be engaged in the same pursuit.

Just as Indian politics of the future can no longer remain isolated or confined to any one communal unit, so the history of the Indian nation of the future is going to be a united whole, in which all individual units will have to merge themselves. Such a history has to take note of the strong and weak points, of the services and disservices, of every separate community, creed or caste, and has to mould them into a solid unit, in which all can take pride and which will supply to all, inspiration and useful lessons derived from past experience. To this common task each nationality of India ought to give the best that it can offer. The days are long past, for any community to emphasize its own individual doings ; we have now to think, as I have said, of India as a whole ; we have all to look upon her as a common mother, for whose honour we have to labour with zeal. Those who do not think in terms of a united India, have no room in the Indian nation of the future.

I am stressing this point purposely to show the severe and inexorable needs of historical research all round. This is not a task for one individual only, nor even for one community or language. All the languages and communities of India must add their own quota to make up this whole. This aspect of history does not seem to have been clearly grasped by us all. We are apt to belittle what others have done and make too much of our own doings. But each community's own past, whether glorious or gloomy, is ultimately essential only in so far as it serves this main purpose of a united national history. There is hardly any country or nation on the face of the earth, which has not jarring sects or divisions in it ; but they have all united for a common purpose and have achieved grand objects in mutual co-operation. The substantial unity of the Indian mind is often lost sight of, in the ardent desire to emphasize differences and divisions. Not only have the Hindus of India a common heritage to boast of, but even the Muhammadans, the Parsees and the Christians living in India have, under the stress of hard reality and time, had such a closely intermixed social life to lead that, for all practical purposes, they taken together even now form a united whole. Only we must accustom ourselves to thinking in this vein, and that is what history is meant to teach us all. In this common life of a united India, our history has to play its part, and that is why I have stressed this point.

3. *Fortunate lead given by two eminent scholars of two distinct types, Sarkar and Rajwade.*

But the needs of historical research and its possible services in this common task of nation-building, seem only recently to have been clearly understood or generally recognized. Some 50 years ago Elliot and Dowson translated into English only a few portions of a number of Persian chronicles, upon which the Muhammadan period of Indian history has been mainly based. During the last half century there have been various attempts in all provinces to collect old historical materials, letters, documents, chronicles, coins, seals, pictures, epigraphs, sculptures and other sources that can elucidate past events. So far as modern India is concerned, two indefatigable workers, more than any others, have shown the right method of research, each in his own way,—Jadunath Sarkar in the north, and the late V. K. Rajwade in the south, although both of them have been more or less misrepresented or misunderstood. Those who closely follow their writings, their methods, and their treatment, have realized the immense advance in historical criticism and spirit, which these two eminent scholars have made in this subject. It was a fortunate coincidence for the history of India, that these two able workers could be found to tackle the problem not only from two different view-points, but also from the two main regional sources,—Sarkar presenting the northern side and Rajwade finding out the Marathi materials and presenting the southern side. Their previous equipment for the task was also, fortunately, entirely different. Sarkar, after a brilliant university career, acquired the experience of training students in colleges and universities; Rajwade, imbued with an innate fire of the heart, which his university career served rather to kindle than to damp, devoted himself, after graduation,-entirely to the service of national history. He taught himself the various subjects essential for historical research, such as the ancient and modern history of Europe and the world, comparative grammar, philology and epigraphy. Although working independently of each other and in different directions, they fortunately happened to concentrate their efforts on the common ground of Maratha history. Prof. Sarkar having taken Aurangzeb for his special study, was required to explore the period of Shivaji and work at it from original Marathi sources, which, I am glad to say, he has mastered with great zeal and profit. This coincidence we must certainly bless with all our heart.[1]

1. Sarkar alone by his *History of Aurangzeb*, his *Shivaji and his*

It was the casual finding of a chronicle (*Bakhar*) of Shivaji's life in the early seventies of the last century, which led to a criticism of Grant Duff's monumental work at the hands of the late Justice Ranade and his colleagues. It was then discovered that many useful *Bakhars* and papers of historical interest existed in different places, which, if published, would not only correct the mistakes of Grant Duff, but would make a substantial addition to his history. Along with the historical papers many original manuscripts of poems and compositions of old Maratha authors, were also discovered. A band of young workers, mostly teachers in high schools, undertook to edit and publish them in a monthly magazine devoted to poetry and history. Thus the *Kavyetihasa-Sangraha* was born in 1878. The last of those enthusiastic workers happily survives to this day, Rao Bahadur Kashinath Narayan Sane,[1] now aged 75 whose scholarship and devotion to the cause of Maratha history are quite well known in my part of the country. This magazine continued for 12 years and published some thirty volumes of historical materials, mostly chronicles, and one or two containing original letters and documents of rare value.

4. *Rajwade.*

This publication, however, did not rouse any keen interest in history in the public mind; it died for want of support. The credit of creating such an interest belongs most certainly to Vishwanath Kashinath Rajwade, now over sixty,[2] who is still carrying on his work, not in the modern but in the ancient period of India. With no means or money of his own, he, after leaving college, started a personal house to house search for papers, not only in

Times, and his *Fall of the Mughal Empire* (4 vols.), has practically reconstructed the history of the whole Maratha period. Other Indian scholars have no doubt contributed to particular fields of Indian history, but as I am dealing with Maharastra only, I do not include these in my review.

1 He died on 17 March 1927.

2 Born July 1864, died 31 Dec. 1926.

big historic cities like Poona, Satara, Nasik and Wai, but went on foot from village to village, tracing old Maratha families of Sardars, clerks and priests, and examining the stock of their papers, on which he pored with a concentration and devotion hardly to be met with in ordinary life. Without heeding hunger or thirst, living on charity and accepting from kindly people gifts of money just enough to satisfy the bare needs of his travel, he roamed about for years, throughout Maharastra and through many parts outside, with heavy loads of old manuscript papers on his back, which he has now stored in different centres with friends and pupils, whom he collected round himself. His selfless devotion was so catching, that bands of intelligent and earnest workers soon gathered round him and helped to collect, store, read, sift, copy, print and publish the papers which came into their hands. Indeed, Rajwade is a fine example of a recluse, *Brahmachari* and *Sanyasi*, showing what one man can do, if he but determinedly applies himself to a self-imposed task, regardless of difficulties and undaunted by want of funds. His collection is now housed at Dhulia.

Rajwade not only collected heaps of useful papers from unsuspected quarters, but showed what precious materials existed in private papers and account books, in sanads and documents of charities, in judicial decisions and personal diaries, which till then used to be considered as practically useless. The size and quality of any old paper, its make, the source from which it came, the kind of writing that it contained, and various other features of a like character, yielded most unsuspected results when handled with the trained skill of Rajwade. On his own initiative he has printed and published till now 22 volumes, each of about 350 pages of original papers, with learned introductions which, although not necessarily related to the subject of the printed papers, discussed various outstanding problems of history in general, and of Maratha history in particular, and imparted valuable guidance on the science, meaning and interpretation of human history and the origin of thought and language.

Rajwade has brought out not only useful old papers, but reconstructed from them Maratha history of all periods, and in its various branches. His dissertations on the origin of human thought and progress, his theories of the origin of scripts and of the Marathi language, his scholarly contributions to the development of social and political life in the various periods of Indian history, such as the Aryan colonization of Maharastra, will ever prove valuable guides to all students of the subject, although further study may disprove many of his theories. He directs his keen eyes without fear, from the Vedas down to the Peshwas. You read his voluminous writings, and you are impressed with wonder by his massive intellect as it attacks intricate problems. With the aid of old papers, copperplates, inscriptions and philology, he handles the subject of historical research with a thoroughness peculiar to himself. His penetrating genius, his single-minded devotion, his tremendous sacrifice of worldly comforts and honours, entitle him to everlasting gratitude from his countrymen. An austere scholar by temperament and choice, and with no other interest in life, Rajwade is nothing if not strong, strong in his mind, strong in his body, strong in his convictions and strong even in his prejudices, of which he has many. Had he been as accurate a guide as he is a brilliant interpreter, he would verily have been the supreme leader of historical scholarship in India.

Rajwade's miscellaneous writings and investigations amount to some ten volumes more. On a rough calculation I can say, that he has brought out some 15,000 printed pages, without burdening any single person, all on his own initiative and resource. His writings are, however, heavy and uncouth, and never take account of the convenience or capacity of his readers. He would not cater to the taste of any one. His long prefaces and discussions come in anywhere, in any volume, which the ordinary student will often find it very difficult to follow. But when they are carefully studied, they will certainly repay the labour bestowed upon them. They evince not only high scholarship but also slashing criticism.

5. *Parasnis.*

Rajwade's example soon attacked other workers to the field. The late Rao Bahadur D. B. Parasnis of Satara has rendered service to this cause, which ranks second only to Rajwade's, and which perhaps proves of greater immediate service to the student in dealing with past events. Not boasting of a high or university education, but gifted with a brilliant memory and untiring energy, Parasnis did his work, also entirely on his own resources, and collected papers, rare books, pictures, and other materials, which go to form what is popularly known as the Historical Museum of Satara, now handed over to Government as a trust for public use.* While Rajwade did his work independently of Government, Parasnis utilized Governmental help and co-operation to the utmost extent. He, too, has printed some 40 volumes of materials in the monthly magazines named *Bharatvarsha* and *Itihasa-Sangraha* which would amount, I think, on a rough calculation, to some 15,000 pages, the main portion of which consists of the *Daftar* or records of the famous Maratha politician Nana Phadnis, after whose death they came to be located in his house at Menavli at the foot of the Mahabaleshwar hills.

6. *Khare.*

Another scholar of a different type and preparation, but equally devoted to study and work, the late Vasudev Vaman Shastri Khare, employed as a Sanskrit teacher at the Miraj High school, found useful papers with the Patwardhan Sardar family of Miraj (in southern Maharastra), dealing with the latter half of the 18th century. He made a wise selection of them and annotated and published them with well arranged and suggestive introductions. He has up to now 14 volumes of 600 pages each to his credit. Khare's genius, not taking high flights like Rajwade's proves immediately more useful to the average student. His son has now published the 15th volume.

The Indian Historical Records Commission appointed by the Government of India and holding its sittings at

* This Museum was removed to Poona in 1939.

different centres, is also the outcome of the keen interest that Government have taken in this national subject. The individual attempts mentioned above were supplemented by the Government of Bombay who had in their possession heaps of old Marathi and English records, located in the Bombay Secretariat and at the Alienation Office in Poona. The last contains what they call the *Peshwas' Daftar*, from which selections were made, and nine good volumes of correspondence and other papers, printed by Parasnis with suitable brief notices in English at the bottom of each page. These are known as the *Peshwas' Diaries*. But the *Peshwas' Daftar* is an enormous store of old papers mostly administrative and some historical, and contains over 27,000 bundles in the Marathi language and the Modi script, and about 8,000 files in English. Government recently instituted a thorough investigation of these records and have printed several thousand letters with foot-notes in English. The work has been of immense benefit to Maratha history. A useful handbook or guide to these records has also been issued by the Bombay Government, who have now offered ample facilities to genuine students to inspect the records on the spot.

7. *B. I. S. Mandal of Poona*

But considering that individual efforts were not sufficient to create the proper historical spirit in the public mind, Rajwade long ago suggested that we should have small bodies of scholars and workers, formed in every principal town of Maharastra and outside, with a view to making a thorough search of the historical materials existing in the region and collecting, discussing and publishing them at convenience so as to secure their ultimate co-ordination. Such a network of historical societies would certainly have been most fruitful, but the suggestion was not widely taken up, except in a few places like Poona, Satara, Dhulia, Baroda, Indore and others. The *Bharata Itihasa Sanshodhaka Mandal* of Poona has, however, earned a great reputation among them all. It has to its credit over a thousand paying members of various grades, a good fireproof building, and over 30 volumes of printed material, with a fairly large store of old papers and critical essays and notices. The scope of the *Mandal* is very wide as its proud name shows. It has devoted its labours not only to history, but to linguistic studies as well, by attending to the collection of old poetry, folk-lore and country ballads, which occupy more than half its printed pages. But the most conspicuous service of the *Mandal* consists not so much in bringing out fresh materials, as in discussing at its fortnightly and yearly meetings, and threshing out innumerable knotty questions and problems, ascertaining their minute details, determining dates and incidents, by sifting the available evidence, and thus settling a good many controversies.

The careers of Shivaji, his mother, father and grandfather, and their various affairs have been closely scrutinized and an amount of useful information has been brought out bearing on those dim earlier times. The fortuitous find by the late Lokamanya Tilak of that rare document known as the *Jedhe Shakavali*, has given a more definite shape to the life and chronology of Shivaji and his movements. The *Mandal* lacks popular support, particularly of the monied classes ; many poor research workers in the Deccan are struggling against the want of funds, and if sufficient money were forthcoming, there would be a rapid and valuable addition to the stock of the *Mandal*'s publications. It has also suffered in publicity, owing to its work being carried on only in Marathi, which cannot reach those who do not know that language. The Dhulia school of workers first directed their energies mostly to the literature of the Ramdasi sect, which only partially touches the main historic current of the Marathas, although very intensive in its character. They have now erected a building where the materials collected by Rajwade have been preserved and offered for study. They issue a quarterly magazine in Marathi called the *Sanshodhak* and print materials collected by Rajwade.

All these publications and those of other individual workers will, I think, amount to altogether some 300 printed volumes or about one lac of pages in Marathi, and nearly a quarter as much may be existing in a printed form in Persian, English and other languages, mostly concerned with Maratha history. With the help of a few friends, I once counted some 300 printed books all bearing on the subject. This appears as a tremendously huge bulk; but what its real nature is, and what kind of service it has done, are questions on which I think I must say a few words. The history of the Shivaji period, which I may roughly date from 1600 to 1707, has undergone almost a new construction. The careers of Shivaji and his ancestors have now come to be entirely reshaped, with full and authentic details, since we are now on a much firmer foundation of fact than about 30 years ago. The credit of this goes mainly to Sir Jadunath Sarkar outside Maharastra, since, without him, the Persian sources and the European records would not have been first brought into use; but the credit equally goes to a devoted band of village to village workers, belonging to the *Bharata Itihasa Mandal* of Poona, of whom Rajwade was the pioneer. Sir Jadunath Sarkar has recently discovered in the archives of Jaipur very valuable contemporary papers bearing on the life of Shivaji and his successors and news-letters from the Mughal Court. Sarkar is now busy in publishing these in a suitable form in his most recent publication *The House of Shivaji*.

The next period of Maratha history viz., from 1707 to 1800, which can be roughly called the Peshwa period, has also been worked over. The first half, that is, up to the battle of Panipat in 1761, had till recently but scanty materials. Rajwade's first seven volumes made it possible to rearrange this period, for which Irvine's *Later Mughals*, Vols. 1 and 2, is also partially useful. Dr. Ashirbadilal's *The First Two Nawabs of Oudh* and *Shuja-ud-Daula*, Dr. Khan's *Nizam-ul-Mulk*, Dr. Raghubir Sinh's *Malwa in Transition* are a few recent additions on this period. The plentiful materials published from their Poona archives by the Government of Bombay have now come to be carefully studied and co-ordinated towards the construction of a proper history of the first three Peshwas. These selections bring to light many fresh writers and incidents hardly known before. The post-Panipat period has already profuse original materials, and here selection becomes a difficult task, just as the scantiness of the papers in the earlier half of the century obstructs the historian. The ten years' period from the murder of Peshwa Narayan Rao to the Treaty of Salbye, 1773-83, is replete with original papers which, to my surprise, amounted to over 6,000 printed pages, Marathi and English, when I counted them.

The Poona Residency Correspondence Series, the papers of Mahadji Sindia published by Gwalior, the Gulgule Daftar of Kotah and the two volumes of the Satara Historical Society formed from papers in the Satara Museum, are some further sources which a student might usefully note.

As is quite natural, time has made havoc with the older records, while as we approach our own times, there is bound to be a larger mass available. The problem facing us in Maharastra in the immediate future, is not so much that of looking out for fresh materials for collection, as that of selecting, printing and publishing those that have already been discovered and utilizing them for constructing a reliable story from them. There are bound to be some gaps here and there, but they can be filled up as time goes on. So if we have already printed some 300 volumes in Marathi, as many more can be easily and usefully brought out from the heaps yet lying unsorted at Poona, Dhulia, Kotah and other places, not to mention some individual possessions which still remain untapped.

8. *Sardesai*

Of all the printed volumes of materials those of Khare only have been carefully arranged and annotated, while those of Rajwade and Parasnis have been published in a scrappy haphazard manner ; hence, to read, classify, index, and arrange them in the chronological order and according to subjects, is a task which I undertook and which I have by now completed, in my eight volumes of the *Marathi Riyasat*, from the beginning up to the year of the extinction of the Maratha power in 1818. I am at present working on the Peshwa period of Maratha history, revising my original Marathi volumes in the light of the fresh materials published from the *Peshwa Daftar*.[1] I have so far done all my work in Marathi and I could not help it as the original papers exist mostly in Marathi. Some of Rajwade's most important papers appear in his volumes 1, 3, 6 and 8,[2]—which are unfortunately now out of print. As a rule Marathi documents bear no dates or the names of the writers and the addresses. I had to read and arrange all these to make a list of places, persons and incidents, find out the correct dates of them from such references or clues as may be existing in their contents ; and when they were arranged in this way, they began to relate a story of their own. I therefore did not concern myself so much with hunting out fresh papers, as with utilizing those that had already been printed. This gave me the chance of studying the whole course of Maratha history, disclosed by original sources. While Rajwade, Parasnis, Khare and other scholars were doing immense labour in finding out and publishing new papers, they could not have a connected picture of the whole Maratha history before their eyes. They were too much preoccupied with particular incidents or periods to spare attention for the whole. In fact their energies were taken up, in the first place, in reading the old Marathi manuscripts, which is not at all an easy task. They are invariably written in the old Modi hand, which changed from time to time. Rajwade is about the only expert in reading Modi of the earlier days. One has to read a paper of that age more than a dozen times, sometimes to show it to various other people in order to see if they could decipher some of the difficult words or letters correctly. The letters usually bear no date, sometimes only the day and the month. It is only the official *sanads* and formal

---

1 I have been issuing revised editions of my Riyasats and have so far reached the end of Shahu's reign. Further work is being withheld by the difficulties of printing.

2 Rajwade's vol. 8 containing papers from the Amatya Daftar has been reprinted by the Amatya of Bavda and is available in the market.

State papers, which bear the date in three eras, the Muslim, the Shalivahana Shaka, and the era introduced by Shivaji at his coronation in the year 1674. But the usual class of private news-letters, concerning a thousand happenings all over the country, are as a rule without date, often the addressees and the writers are not at all mentioned, often also the top and the bottom have perished, and some are found mutilated. Heaps of such mutilated papers have been printed by Rajwade, which to an ordinary reader would not be clear, but as I had from the beginning made indexes of persons, dates, events, places and other references, I found I was able to decipher most of the mutilated papers from their contents or from their tenor, and I could fix nearly all the dates accurately, or at any rate, approximately. The *Patren Yadi* volume of the *Kavyetihasa-Sangraha,* as also the recently published *Aitihasik Patravyavahar*, are indeed the most important, and are now properly edited and reprinted with all the corrected dates and other necessary references. In fact my original copies of most of these books have all been marked, and I have been urged by many scholars to print and publish all the verified dates and other corrections, for the benefit of future students, but I cannot spare time for this useful work just now. With the greatest difficulty I have been able to prepare and publish a sort of working index of the two great printed collections, I mean, those of Parasnis and of the B. I. Mandal of Poona, together with a complete list of all printed books, dealing with Maratha history, with the necessary details about them that a research student is likely to require.[1] I am mentioning all this, in order to convey to all workers outside an idea as to the kind of work we have been doing in Maharastra. The process requires a lot of correspondence, and one has also to be watching carefully for outside lectures, discussions or articles of historical interest, that are published in the various magazines and news-

---

1 These printed indexes were available for a nominal price with the Pant Pratinidhi of Aundh, Dist. Satara ; and the list of books is sold by K. B. Dhawale, book-seller, Bombay 4, for 2 as. per copy. But all copies are now sold away.

papers all over the country. With all my labour I cannot claim to be exhaustive or complete. I must have lost sight of many useful points. My studies have grown on me, and even the indexes to my own notes are daily increasing, beyond the working powers of one man. Nor can I utilize the help of others in this task, because all the papers must, after all, pass through one brain, in order to secure uniformity of method and interpretation. There is unfortunately no division of labour possible under Indian conditions. The toils of writers are not here shared by the publishers, as is done in Europe. I have to be my own clerk, copyist, record-keeper, often my own printer and publisher and often also the financier. My only consolation is, that many brother students are struggling like me at this time with similar difficulties, and this is the way in which we can all help one another. I draw your attention to all this, in order that we may secure as much co-ordination as possible between the scattered efforts and agencies, that are engaged in this national task all over the country, particularly outside Maharastra.

India is a continent containing several languages which all have more or less old historical materials. We at present need representative scholars of each nationality, working in its own language and publishing their results through a common medium, which, for higher thought and interchange of ideas, is bound to be English for a pretty long time. I am very anxious to present in an English garb not only my past labours but the valuable experience I obtained during my four years' handling of the huge *Peshwas' Daftar* at Poona, so as to make them available to readers not knowing Marathi.[1] There are often traditions, anecdotes, gossips, reports, poems, or bardic songs, from which one has to cull whatever they can yield, always keeping an eye on rigid truth and the human frailties involved in the correct interpretation of past events. That is the way we can all help each other and co-ordinate our labours towards a common object.

---

1 This dream of mine has now been accomplished by the publication of my *New History of the Marathas.*

9. *The spirit actuating a national history,— the task before the nation*

While on this subject, I should like to explain the spirit in which I think a national history should be viewed. Foreign writers are often carried away by unjustifiable prejudices. Even the impartiality of a historian has its limitations. He must remember that he is writing for his own people. He desires their edification, prosperity, well-being. He knows that he must point out national faults gently to correct them, and not depict them severely and unsympathetically, so as to depress them for ever. He must suggest to them their good points, not to make them vain or boastful, but to encourage them to greater and nobler efforts. A historian is in fact to a nation what a father is to his children. Both in reward and punishment, the father has always the good of his children at heart. That is why national histories in all countries have been written by one of the people. We must, of course, know what others have to say of us ; but the sympathetic spirit must run in the vein throughout. For there is none in this world so perfect and faultless, as to be regarded as an oracle, nor none so useless as to be entirely condemned. All national heroes can be presented to the rising generation in whichever colour one likes to paint them. That is why histories written by foreigners and often unquestionably taken as authority by some of our own scholars, are not found to possess the right spirit. There are, of course exceptions and noble exceptions too. I am tempted to give here an instance of how history is often misread. Western writers of the early 19th century have spoken of the Maratha Jagirdars as forming a confederacy of States. But a confederacy means an alliance of independent and equal partners formed for a particular purpose. The Confederacy of Delos is an instance in Greek history, and the *Entente Cordiale* in the first Great War is another. Such a confederacy never existed in the Maratha State. There were doubtless Jagirdars, exercising influence and authority in various parts of India. But they were subject to the central power, first, of the

Chhatrapatis and afterwards, of the Peshwas; and if they disobeyed the Central Government frequently or occasionally, like the Barons of Feudal England, it was because the latter could not enforce obedience. The famous Ahalya Bai Holkar of Indore used to render yearly accounts of receipts and disbursements to the Peshwas right up to her death in 1795. An open defiance of the central authority took place only after the accession of Baji Rao II. to power, as he ceased to be an impartial head of the nation as a whole. Even Mahadaji Sindia never avowedly disobeyed the Peshwa or his agent Nana Phadnis. So the word confederacy has been used by writers for the Jagirdars of this Baji Rao II.'s period. The British then had begun to form independent alliances with them, such as the Bhosles of Nagpur, the Sindia or the Gaikwad, with the avowed object of detaching them from their allegiance to the Peshwa. The Gaikwad was the first to accept the British approaches and to throw off the authority of the Peshwa.

Indian history suffers from other causes also. India has several nationalities, and the want of co-ordination or sympathy between the writers of the various provinces injures the general interests of the nation. A Maratha or a Sikh or a Rajput is very often apt to make too much of his own race and thereby give umbrage to others. This has resulted, as we look around us, in tension and disunion. I think, however, that if we in our historical studies always keep in view the ideal of building up an Indian nationality, out of all the elements that we have about us, we can benefit ourselves by emphasizing the good points that each Indian nationality can put forth on its behalf, from its own past records. We should all ungrudgingly welcome whatever others can say for themselves, provided it is supported by authentic evidence. Indeed, the two main races of India, the Hindu and the Muslim, being in the same boat, have been complements of each other all through their historic past, and are practically indistinguishable from each other except in name. If the idealism of the Hindu and the practical spirit of the Muslim, could join for the service of humanity for which the whole eastern world is crying, the regeneration of the Asiatic races would be greatly facilitated.

Workers in this field have also to bear in mind that no history can be allowed to become stereotyped or stagnant. It has to guide the nation at all times, and hence it requires to be reshaped from time to time, not merely because new facts come to be discovered, but because the new aspects, new situations, new ideals that arise in the life of a society demand fresh treatment in order to supply guidance to leaders and actors; also because the participant in the progress of an age is led to standpoints from which the past can be regarded and judged in a novel manner. On this account a history has always to be growing and is a progressive science in which the changes in the world give to old facts a new significance, and in which every truly penetrating and original mind sees in the old facts something which had not been seen before. Great writers have emphasized this view of history at all times.

I have so far explained to you how we in the south and the west are occupied; we now need the help of the north and the east. I am told there are heaps of Persian papers all over northern India, scattered through many important towns, institutions, and individual families; and many more could be found if a search were made from place to place, by a band of workers like those of Maharastra. If these Persian papers are arranged and published, they will supply a fresh life-story of the northern races and their doings, and supplement or correct what the sources in Marathi, English and other languages have already yielded. In fact, we should get representative workers in each language and trust them to construct their own story from available sources. In this way, we can get together in the best first-hand manner all the historical past of each family, clan or community as presented by their own students. Such separate contributions will ultimately go to form a comprehensive, united and authentic history of India, all from original sources. This is what we have got to do.*

There are heaps of British records also, which we Indians ought to study from our own point of view. The East India Company's records have been printed in numerous volumes and are indeed valuable ; but they do not supply the kind of information that we need for our own history. The Imperial Records in New Delhi and the Records of the several provincial secretariats, await research from Indian scholars. These with the Persian and Marathi records will, when carefully worked. give us an acceptable story.

What we just now need most, is records of the type of the printed volumes of the *Calendar of Persian Correspondence* (Imperial Records Office), for the whole Peshwa period, particularly from 1707 to 1772, in which the Maratha influence attained its greatest expansion. It is a great boon that these Persian Calendars have been made available in English. I know it will be an equal boon to non-Maratha students, if some of the most important Marathi papers are published in English, in order that there may be a real interchange of research, between the two main currents of thought and language in India. But the task of rendering Marathi papers into English is well nigh impracticable, as there are already some 300 volumes available in print, of which I have spoken before. It is only recently that some of the universities have taken up Indian history for post-graduate studies ; if they had started it long ago, the results would certainly have been by now more encouraging. You will thus see what great need there is for an interchange of thought and discussion, if our national history is to be constructed on sure and scientific foundations.

But such a national history to be full and all-sided, must contain information on all topics, of which politics is only one, although doubtless an important portion.

* Such a project for writing the history of the Indian nation is already afoot in the present changing politics of India. Several families in Maharastra have published their own histories.

The Marathi papers contain an enormous amount of useful matter about social, religious, literary, military, industrial, judicial and other topics ; but unless the main currents of political activities have been determined from beginning to end, these other topics cannot be satisfactorily dealt with. A great deal of discussion has already taken place in Maharastra ; and some published books, particularly those of the B. I. Mandal of Poona, contain much information of an all-India character, which will certainly bear translation into English, in order that the other parts of the Indian continent may be enabled to add to or improve upon, what Maharastra has tried to supply. A gentleman of Dhulia once carefully studied the old judicial papers and decisions and published from them a few useful articles upon the legal administration of the Marathas.. Dr. S. N. Sen's *Administrative and Military Systems of the Marathas*, published under the auspices of the Calcutta University, are admirable pioneering attempts in another direction, although the subjects dealt therein are yet in a crude stage, and require being developed in many essentials, upon which fresh investigation is daily throwing light. Students in Indian universities have produced theses on various topics, which are quite useful for a national history.

History as its main object treats of the doings of those great warriors and statesmen who have cut a conspicuous figure in the past, but no national work of the kind could have been accomplished without the willing services and sacrifices of hundreds and thousands of minor persons, possessing more or less ability, and contributing their quota to the main current. Grant Duff and a few other writers of the early 19th century, made only a passing reference to some of the persons and families figuring in Maratha history ; but when I began to scrutinize the heaps of papers now available, I found there were very many great and good names whose deeds history must take note of. I have been thus able to present to the readers a fresh account of over a hundred families, of all castes, with their genealogies, dates and other details, so that when fresh names occur in any paper, we can identify them at once. I have, besides, tried to bring together all personal and social details of those families and their members, who had played any part in Maratha history, in order that we may be able to draw some instructive conclusions, as regards the life of our society and its working in the days when Maharastra was practically enjoying *Swarajya*. If all these hundred families and their genealogies were to be carefully examined, one would deduce much useful information from them,—for instance, what the average working life of men of those days was, how far the conditions were favourable to the increase or decrease of population, what kind of education was in vogue, and how it affected the moral and physical well-being of the nation. In this way only can our national history be slowly constructed.

In my next lectures I shall proceed to discuss some of the main points established by recent research, in order to bring home to you an idea of the vast extent of the work we have yet to do, before we are able to produce an acceptable national history of this vast Indian continent.

LECTURE III

SHIVAJI'S CONCEPTION OF A HINDU EMPIRE

1. *Shivaji takes his cue from his father*

The descent of Shivaji from the solar Sisodia dynasty of Chitor had long been traditionally accepted in Maharastra and has been recently confirmed by the publication in facsimile, of several important Persian sanads held by the late Raja of Mudhol, in the Bijapur district surnamed Ghorpade.* This family of Mudhol and that of the Chhatrapatis of Satara are alleged to have descended from a common ancestor, Sajjansinh, grandson of Rana Lakshmansinh, of Chitor. Sajjansinh migrated to the south about the year 1320 after the terrible havoc wrought upon Chitor by the Pathan Sultan Ala-ud-din Khilji. Sajjansinh, his brother Khemsinh and their successors are said to have served governors in the Bahamani Kingdom and won from them various jagirs at different times, the original deeds of which are now available for study.[1] About the year 1470, two brothers, Karansinh and Shubhakrishna, descendants of Sajjansinh, effected a partition of their landed property ; the former, i.e., the elder, inheriting the southern portion of Mudhol and the younger Shubhakrishna, obtaining the northern portion between Daulatabad and Poona. The Mudhol branch acquired their surname of Ghorpade, for having successfully scaled by means of an iguana (*ghorpad*) the walls of Khelna or Vishalgad under the command of Mahmud Gawan, the famous minister of the Bahamani kings. Maloji Bhosle, the grandfather of Shivaji, was about the

* The authenticity of these Firmans has been seriously questioned. They are said to be spurious.

1 *Shivaji the Great*, Vol. I, pt. I, by Dr. Balkrishna.

fifth in descent from the younger branch represented by Shubhakrishna. It would thus seem that there intervened about twelve generations during the three hundred years that elapsed between Sajjansinh and Maloji (1320-1620). The Bhosles and the Ghorpades, after being once separated, followed different fortunes in their respective careers and often manifested deadly enmity against each other during historic times. We know how Baji Ghorpade was prominent in arresting Shahji Bhosle near Jinji and how he was later on attacked and killed by Shivaji out of revenge. Like the Bhosles and the Ghorpades, it should be noted, several other Maratha families of the Deccan such as the Pawars, the Jadhavs, the Moreys etc., also claim a Rajput origin.

An enormous mass of old Marathi and Persian papers of pre-Shivaji days which have been recently published, throw considerable light on the early activities of Shivaji and his two immediate ancestors Shahji and Maloji. Shahji served with distinction and valour under Malik Ambar, the able minister of the kings of Ahmadnagar. Malik Ambar taking advantage of the guerilla tactics so admirably suited to the hilly regions of western Deccan and so ably employed by the Maratha leaders under Bijapur, Golkonda and Ahmadnagar, successfully resisted for a quarter of a century the persistent efforts of Jahangir to extend his empire into the south.

Several scholars have observed a curious fact in these occurrences, that just as Shivaji and Aurangzeb between them created the history of the latter half of the seventeenth century, so did to some extent before them their fathers also in the earlier part of that century. Shahji (1594-1664) and Shah Jahan (1592-1666), contemporaries in age and activity played a game of war which was later continued by their sons. Their grandfathers Jahangir and Maloji were the first to find themselves in opposition. Lukhji Jadhaorao held an influential position under the Nizam Shah then ruling from Daulatabad and deserted to the Mughals in the early part of the struggle, thereby encountering his son-in-law in open fight more than once. In the battle of Bhatavdi towards the end of 1624 Malik Ambar succeeded with the help of Shahji and other Marathas in inflicting a crushing defeat upon the combined Mughal and Bijapuri armies, mainly by a highly developed method of guerilla warfare. The next three years (1624-1627) were full of trouble both for Shah Jahan and Shahii ; the former rebelled against his father, wandered all over India to find shelter from his father's armies and for nearly a year remained in secret hiding at Junnar, in the vicinity of which Shivaji was born. During the same period 1625-1627 Shahji, disgusted with the treatment he obtained from Malik Ambar, transferred his allegiance to the Adilshah of Bijapur. Both Ibrahim Adilshah and Jahangir died in 1627, and when in a few months Shah Jahan acquired his father's throne, he made two important incursions into the south (Jan. 1631—June 1632, and February to June 1636), using all his imperial resources in completing the task of reducing the Deccan. To this aggressive march of the Emperor, Shahji who had left the service of Bijapur, offered a bold and intrepid opposition for seven years (1629-1636), which later served as a living object lesson, both in warfare and diplomacy, to his son in undertaking grand projects for winning independence for his race and religion. The terrible experiences and indescribable sufferings, which Shivaji's shrewd mother Jijabai had to pass through during that period, left an indelible mark upon the tender mind of Shivaji and inspired him with a spirit hardly equalled in the annals of history. Shahji made Poona the centre of his activities, erected there gardens and houses for his residence, and turned to full advantage the peculiar situation created by nature in that hilly tract known as the Mavals or the land of the setting sun, which extended along the two ridges of the Sahyadri range roughly from Junnar and Kalyan in the north to Wai and Raigad in the south. This difficult tract was hardly ever fully brought under an organized peaceful rule by the Bahamani kings or their successors of Ahmadnagar and Bijapur, and being inhabited by turbulent lords called Deshmukhs, it was something like a no-man's land, a wedge so to say sandwiched between the two kingdoms.

Shah Jahan realizing the difficulties of the situation, wisely retraced his steps after having finally extinguished the last vestiges of Ahmadnagar[1] and expelling Shahji from Maharastra allowed him to enter the service of Bijapur, to carve out for himself a different field of activity in the Karnatak for the rest of his life. It would thus appear that the wonderful career of Shivaji was not a sudden innovation or an accidental eruption like a wild fire of the Sahyadris, as Duff puts it, but the legitimate development of a process first undertaken by Malik Ambar and then ably continued by Shivaji's father, whom the contemporary writers have on that account given the appropriate appellation of a kingmaker. Shivaji's achievements viewed in this light would appear to be only a step onward, his mother shrewdly acting as the connecting link between the father and the son.

2. *Main incidents in Shivaji's career*

It is just as well that I advert here to the main incidents which made Shivaji a remarkable hero of Maharashtra and perhaps of all India. His early life was full of adventure and audacity. Having been, since his birth, practically separated from his father, Shivaji received the necessary training for life at the hands of his mother and his guardian Dadaji Kondadeo and started his unique career among mountain fastnesses, away from the public gaze, by befriending the local landlords, by repairing and capturing old forts and building new ones and reducing to obedience all who defied his authority in his father's jagir.[2] The first significant incident which made him a personality to be reckoned with, was his victory over the Moreys of Javli in 1656. Three years after, mainly by cautious strategy and clever diplomacy, he scored a brilliant success against Afzal Khan, the powerful general of Bijapur, and thereby not only struck terror into the hearts

---

1 The partition treaty is given in Sarkar's *Aurangzeb*, Vol. I.

2 The first ascertained date of the beginning of his eventful career is Ist August 1644 when Dadaji captured Sinhgad, the capital of the western province; and Shivaji's paternal swarajya was complete by 1653.

of all his rivals but established his reputation as a gifted and intrepid hero equal to any emergency. Within the next four years he baffled the efforts of Aurangzeb's generals Jaswantsinh and Shaista Khan to overcome him, made a friendly compromise with the renowned Mirza Raja Jaysinh and upon his advice visited the emperor's Court at Agra in 1666. His open defiance to the all-powerful Emperor and his miraculous escape from captivity, at once brought him an all-India reputation as an irresistible opponent of the Mughal Empire, inspired by Providence for the deliverance of the Hindu nation. Thereafter he continued his career of uninterrupted conquest, and in 1674 had himself formally crowned as an independent king, entitled to all the traditional honours of a Kshatriya. During the next six years of his life he extended his dominions to the mouth of the Kaveri and met with a rather sudden and untimely death in 1680, leaving behind him a splendid legacy to his nation as an unequalled conqueror, the creator and inspiring idol of his nation and the last constructive genius among the Hindus.

I would here like to point out wherein Shivaji's greatness lies and how his example affords practical guidance to leaders of men in all times.

In my opinion the greatness of Shivaji consists in his having transformed the mentality of the Maratha nation, whom by means of his unequalled leadership he enabled to attain to the foremost place among the various races of India. It is well known what a factious, turbulent and riotous life the Maratha clans of the western hills led for over a century before the rise of Shivaji. They had been wasting their energy in internecine disputes obeyed no authority and made life and property hopelessly insecure. Shivaji correctly gauged the situation, heartily joined them, to begin with, in their lawless activities and having quickly gained their confidence, established such a complete hold upon their contentious and valiant spirit that they began to render implicit obedience to him and put forth a united national effort in defence of their country's liberty. The roving undisciplined bands soon came to realize the value of willing comradeship and followed their leader in weal and woe. The Maratha name thus came to be respected and feared throughout India within the short period of about twenty years. Shivaji ultimately laid the formal legal foundation of the Maratha Raj and after a brief but brilliant career left behind an example of a unique constructive genius, bringing about the necessary solidarity among scattered and warring elements.

We Indians in our present troubles of discord and disunion, have much to learn from this brilliant example. Let us hope it will inspire us.

3. *Influence of Ramdas and other saints*

As it is necessary for us to understand what the Maratha policy was and how it changed from time to time, we must go back and ascertain from documentary evidence the original aim of Shivaji when he undertook the task of establishing an independent Maratha kingdom. Whether Shivaji contemplated the establishment of a Hindu empire for all the various peoples of India, or whether he confined his attention only to a small kingdom of his own in Maharastra, is a point on which opinions have differed rather sharply. I should, therefore, like to put down what decision I have been able to come to, on this question, after taking into account the available evidence. From a small *Jagir* of his father confined almost to some two taluks of the present day, *i.e.*, from Junnar to Supa, Shivaji, before his death in 1680, extended his Raj, as I have said, roughly from the western sea to the river Bhima on the east, and from the Tapti in the north to the Kaveri in the south. I have already shown that Shivaji stood forth as the champion of the Hindu religion : it was to protect his religion that he started his campaigns in antagonism to Muslim aggression. In ascertaining the aim of Shivaji, we must take particular note of the surrounding atmosphere in which he was born and bred, and which has been amply reproduced in the contemporary writings of the Indian saints, who spoke of politics in terms of religion. These saints had realized that all north India was levelled to the ground under the

Muhammadan yoke; and the work of regeneration was undertaken by Shivaji in the south, calling himself a champion of Hinduism. Most of these saints had travelled far and wide throughout India and freely mixed with the peoples of different places, had seen and observed the sufferings of the Hindus, the destruction of their temples, sacred objects and holy places, and, in their own way, freely discussed what measures could possibly be taken to remedy this state of things and defend their religion.

Ramdas, born 20 years before Shivaji and surviving him by two years, started his own independent movement for religious regeneration by establishing Ramdasi *maths* or convents in various places, and helping in his own way the efforts of the political leaders as much as possible. It is said that Ramdas established throughout India in all about 800 *maths*, of which some 72 have been known as more important. His teaching had great influence right up to the southernmost point of India. In the province of Tanjore in the far south, the sect of Ramdas had a large following, and for 200 years after him, there was a considerable addition to the Marathi literature from this Tanjore section of Ramdas's followers. A number of poems, dictionaries, grammars, dramas, ballads and chronicles, came to be written in Marathi in the province of Tanjore, whose kings themselves were great patrons of learning and took a large personal share in these productions. The results are deposited in the Saraswati Mandir at that town. Ananda-Tanaya and Raghunath Pandit are famous among the Marathi poets of Tanjore, and are known as the followers of Ramdas's teachings. There, on the stone walls of the temple of Brihadishwar, was carved, in the early 19th century, a Marathi inscription in bold, beautiful Devanagri characters, narrating the whole history of the Maratha kingdom of Tanjore, which is now reproduced in some 130 pages of a book in small print. Such a large historical inscription is nowhere else to be found in the whole world. At the time of Shivaji's death there were in Maharastra about 1200 followers of the Ramdasi cult. This large number of one particular type, working for the uplift of the country, strikes one as a grand creation of Ramdas, influencing the popular mind in shaping the future destiny of Maharastra.

Ramdas's own writings are vivacious and penetrating and breathe an intense national spirit in every expression. They are comprehensive, dealing with every phase of practical life and meticulously inculcate the virtues of truth, devotion and self-reliance. Styling himself *samarth* or powerful, Ramdas stood for an all round national regeneration and the conservation of the physical and moral resources of the people. They began to assemble in the *maths* where they were profoundly impressed by the teachings of Ramdas as expounded in his great work, the *Dasa-Bodha* (Advice to a slave,) which is supposed to have led the people to help the national work of Shivaji. They soon imbibed the underlying principles of Shivaji's moves, as day after day they began to be crowned with success. What particular work was entrusted to these *maths* from the point of view of political propaganda is not definitely on record ; and it is even questioned how far Ramdas's teaching actually helped the national uplift. Each *math* had a temple of Rama and Hanuman with, we presume, several gymnasiums or *akhadas* attached to them, so that the main work of these *maths* must have been to build up and conserve the physical and moral strength of the people. As the *Dasa-Bodha* grew up from day to day, it began to be read and studied in these *maths,* having far reaching effects upon society in general. Ramdas urged that institutions small and big should be formed in all quarters, in order to increase the strength of the nation in every possible way. Large congregations used to assemble at the *maths* to hear the sermons, and we know that most of the prominent associates of Shivaji accepted the Ramdasi cult and followed his teachings. Thus, in the movement for Swaraj, Shivaji is supposed to represent the physical and Ramdas the moral force of the nation. Shivaji had appropriated the traditional diplomacy, warfare, philosophy and arts of old Vijayanagar and incorporated them into his own fresh ideal ; and Ramdas with his experience and travel, adopted for the acceptance of his nation the important tenets of the teachings of Nanak, Kabir, Chaitanya and Tukaram. the great saints of India. The only difference between the two was that Ramdas was intensely practical, straightforward, outspoken and comprehensive. There is a burning fire and force in every word of his. Shivaji from the beginning mixed very freely with all classes of people, and felt particular reverence for Ramdas and other saints and learned men, who had gained experience of the world. Both doubtless possessed high aims, but one may well doubt how far they pursued their aims in conscious co-operation. Shivaji's father and mother were already chafing under Muslim subjection, and constantly thought of measures for defending their religion and their country. There is no positive evidence to prove that Ramdas directly inspired Shivaji in his political moves or ideals.

4. *The coronation ceremony and its purpose.*

Secondly, Shivaji's wars and campaigns, his plans and movements, and his words and arrangements, throughout his brilliant career of some thirty-five years, when minutely examined, do not in the least show that he had restricted his vision to Maharastra or the Deccan only. He did not know that his life was going to be cut short by an untimely death ; it could easily have been lengthened by at least another twenty years, even if fate did not vouchsafe him the ripe old age which his opponent Aurangzeb reached. Shivaji's foundations were broad enough to sustain an all-India edifice, to which his measures unmistakably pointed. The coronation ceremony, which he deliberately carried out with unprecedented magnificence under the direction of a scion of the celebrated Bhatta family of Benares, was of the truly ancient Kshatriya type of the *Ashwamedha* days, imitating the rites and splendour of an Ashoka, a Samudragupta, or a Harsha-Vardhana. Shivaji had his ancient pedigree established through the Kshatriya family of Chitor, who claimed their descent from Sri Ramchandra. The significant titles which Shivaji assumed *viz., Kshatriya-Kulavatansa, Sinhasanadhishwara, Chhatrapati,* his avowed profession of the protection of cows and Brahmans as his goal, the eloquent motto on his official seal so thoughtfully composed, his deliberate adoption of Sanskrit synonyms for Persian Court terms, his acceptance of Marathi as the Court language and his translation into practice of the old *Shastric* injunctions about the eight ministers and their duties, as also his avowed acceptance of the system of the four castes in which he claimed for himself the position of a Kṣhatriya, all these clearly point to a pan-Hindu ideal which would have been out of place for a small Maratha kingdom confined to the Deccan, following more or less the type of one of the branches of the Bahamani Empire.

Thirdly, Shivaji's method of establishing and expanding a small independent kingdom, gives in itself a clue to his future aims, *viz* his imposition of the two claims of the *Sardeshmukhi* and the *Chauthai,* of which I am going to speak a little later. The former he claimed from the Emperor Shahjahan as early as 1648, as hereditary *Watan* due to his position as a Sardeshmukh or head territorial officer among the Maratha nation ; while the latter he revived about the year 1660 when he conquered the north Konkan, where the kings of Ramnagar used to exact it from the surrounding districts. From the beginning, he skilfully forged these two convenient weapons as a serviceable means to enable his people, in the long run, to establish a Hindu empire throughout the Indian continent.

5. *Befriending other Hindu princes*

Fourthly, whenever the Emperor or other Muhammadan kings were at war with Shivaji, he took care to differentiate between his various opponents. He never fought, as a rule, the Hindu generals of the Emperor. He tried to be friendly to Jashvantsinh and openly won over Jaysinh, both Rajputs of high descent, to whom Shivaji showed great regard. A letter in Persian verse, supposed to have been written by Shivaji to Jaysinh, has been published by Babu Jagannath Das in the *Nagari-Pracha-*

rini Patrika. It purports to mention Shivaji's objects in clear and emphatic terms. Even if the authenticity of the letter be questioned, we may presume, it gives us a faithful idea conveyed in poetical terms, of what the general impression prevailing at the time was, as regards the venture undertaken by Shivaji in opposing the Emperor. It also reflects the actual state of things at the time. "O Great King," says Shivaji in the letter, "though you are a great Kshatriya, you have been using your strength to increase the power of the dynasty of Babar. You are shedding the blood of the Hindus, in order to make the red-faced Muslims victorious. Do you not realize that you are thereby blackening your reputation before the whole world? If you have come to conquer me, I am ready to lay down my head in your path; but since you come as the Deputy of the Emperor, I am utterly at a loss to decide how I should behave towards you. If you fight on behalf of the Hindu religion, I am ready to join and help you. You are brave and valiant, it behoves you as a powerful Hindu prince, to take the lead against the Emperor. Let us go and conquer Delhi itself. Let us shed our costly blood to preserve our ancient religion and give satisfaction to our thirsty ancestors. If two hearts can combine, they will break down any amount of hard resistance. I bear no enmity to you and do not wish to fight with you. I am ready to come and meet you alone. I will then show you the secret letter which I have snatched out of the pocket of Shayista Khan. If you do not accept my terms, my sword is ready."

Similarly one Ratnakar Bhatt, almost a contemporary of Shivaji, has composed a Sanskrit poem describing the kings of Jaipur, in which he thus writes about Mirza Raja Jaysinh (1621-1667) whom Aurangzeb had employed to subjugate Shivaji. "Mirza Raja,"* says the author,

---

* येन-श्रीजयसिंहेन दिल्लीन्द्रपदलिप्सवः ।
शिवप्रभृतिभूपाला वशं नीताः स्वतेजसा ॥
—ग्रंथमाला, राजवाडे सं. लेख, जयपुर वंशावळ.

"displayed great valour in conquering Shivaji and other kings who desired to *capture the imperial seat of Delhi.*" Many have taken this as a contemporary impression of Shivaji's aspirations.

I have no time to quote many such letters here : one written by Shivaji to Emperor Aurangzeb on the subject of the Jazia is very eloquent, and can be read in translation in Prof. Sarkar's *Shivaji*. Shivaji's letters to his brother and his letter to Maloji Ghorpade son of the murdered Baji Ghorpade, clearly set forth the objects he was trying to attain and must convince all doubters about the sincerity of his purpose. They contain sentiments which eminently establish Shivaji's object of the *Hindu-pad-Padshahi*. His brother Ekoji held himself to be a subordinate and jagirdar of the Adilshah of Bijapur, which Shivaji would not tolerate. He would not allow Ekoji to be either an independent ruler or subordinate to Bijapur, as his scheme of a Hindu empire would not brook such a position. That is why Shivaji had to lead an expedition against Ekoji, and humble him into obedience. He offered Ekoji a jagir in the Deccan. Writes he to his brother : "God out of His grace assigned to me a mission. He has entrusted to me an all-India empire (*Sarva-bhauma Rajya*). He has given me the strength to crush the Muslims, whose shelter you have sought. How can you succeed against me, and how can you save the Muslims ? If you follow my advice, well and good ; if not, you will surely have to repent." In his letter to Maloji Ghorpade Shivaji says : "I have formed a league of all Maratha chiefs with the object of preserving their estates, in order that we should be masters in our own home : that we should preserve or destroy Muslim kingdoms at our pleasure. My effort is solely directed towards bringing all the Marathas together and making them strong. Why are you so much in love with the foreign Bijapur kingdom ? It is already reduced to dust. What can the Bijapur king give you, and why do you parade your loyalty to a Muslim king ? That Pathan is not going to benefit you in any way. We Marathas have already swallowed them up. You must remember that you are a Maratha, and that my object is to unite and raise you all into a strong nation."

It is doubtless clear that Shivaji had in his vision the old Kshatriya races and their achievements in northern India, such as the Guptas, the Chalukyas, the Rastrakutas and the Yadavas. The Bundela king Chhatrasal was his friend, and came to the Deccan to seek his advice. Northern bards and poets specially came to Shivaji's Court after his escape from Agra, and received his patronage. All this points to the all-India character of Shivaji's undertaking.

But this ideal was rather religious than political. The essential object of Shivaji's and his followers' system was to earn complete freedom for Hindu religious practices, without persecution or interference from the Muslims. There was never an intention of having a Hindu Emperor on the throne of Delhi. Chimnaji Appa fighting at Bassein against the Portuguese, or Sadashivrao Bhau at Panipat against Abdali, was actuated by the same religious motive of freeing India from the iconoclastic spirit of the foreigners. A Sanskrit letter addressed by Shivaji's son Sambhaji to Raja Ram Singh of Jaipur has been discovered recently in the archives of Jaipur which clearly mentions his ideal of religious freedom. It is noteworthy in this connection to remember that while the Marathas exercised political supremacy in India, that is right up to the close of the 18th century, no Hindu potentate cared to seek British protection. It is the four Muslim Nawabs, viz. those of Arcot, Bengal, Oudh and Haidarabad who first sought British help and strengthened the British power in India during the latter half of the 18th century. They sold India's freedom before others.*

6. *All-India travel and experience*

Fifthly, Shivaji himself visited northern India, when he went to meet the Emperor at Agra. He purposely

* See Jaipur letters in *House of Shivaji* by Sir J. N. Sarkar.

undertook this visit and had no compulsion for it from the Emperor. He utilized the occasion in studying the situation in the far north and the imperial capital. Before starting, he coolly weighed the pros and cons of the undertaking with Jaysinh. In his interview with that prince, Shivaji had come to form certain plans which his movements thereafter confirm. Shivaji did strongly wish to see for himself what the Emperor and his Court were like, wherein their strength lay, and how he should thereafter deport himself so as to encompass his aims. To realize this fully, he made up his mind to proceed to the Emperor's Court. He left Raigad on 5th March 1666, reached Agra on 12th May, escaped from confinement on 17th August and reached home on 20th November. His marvellous escape from the imperial custody is too well-known to be described here. On his return journey from Agra he visited Mathura, Brindavan, Ayodhya, Prayag, Benares and other holy places. Returning home after an absence of eight months, he had utilized the interval in seeing the whole country, talking to all kinds of people, and gaining valuable experience, of which he made full use afterwards. This shows that Shivaji's plan included an all-India movement. This does not, of course, mean that he wished at once to have himself crowned as the Emperor of Delhi : that was impossible then. But his idea was ultimately to establish a Hindu Empire of suzerain power for all India, gradually expanding it from its original base in the Deccan. Had he lived long enough, one feels sure, he would have achieved his object.

7. *Measures for uniting Maratha elements*

There are many other points of minor importance, contained in the papers of those times, which confirm the view I have taken. Shivaji's trip to Golconda, his conquest of the Karnatak, and his expedition to Tanjore against his brother, are simply links in the grand unifying chain of imperial aims, which become clear when the links are properly arranged. Shivaji always took care to win over his own Deccani Marathas such as the Jedhes and the

Bandals, with affectionate sympathy and goodwill. He did not hesitate, however, to inflict severe punishments on those who, like the Moreys and the Khopdes, dared to oppose his aims. He married eight wives with a set purpose and not out of mere whim or pleasure. In those days of social inequalities, he contracted these marriage connections in order to link together by matrimonial alliances many Kshatriya families of the Deccan, as the Bhosles were by no means considered at the time high enough in popular estimation. Bajaji Nimbalkar, who had been compelled to accept the Muslim faith by the Adilshah, was re-admitted to the Hindu fold by Shivaji, who then gave his own daughter in marriage to Bajaji's son. Of all Maratha families the Moreys were the only ones whom he handled rather severely; otherwise, he fought with no Hindu general and made friends with Hindu statesmen at foreign Courts, such as Madanna and Akanna of Golconda. It must, however, be clearly understood that although Shivaji's highest aim was to uphold the Hindu religion, he had no ill feeling towards the Muhammadans as a religious community or towards Muslim kingdoms, if they would show the same reverence to the Hindu religion as they did to their own. He considered himself a protector of all faiths and sects, and treated all of them equally. He, as we know, gave *Inam* lands and annuities to Muslim shrines and institutions. He revered the saint Baba Yakut of Kelsi as much as he did Ramdas. He had faithful Muhammadans in his own service, occupying high posts of trust and honour, like Qazi Haidar whom Aurangzeb afterwards appointed as Chief Justice at Delhi. When Shivaji was a captive of the Emperor at Agra, his life was saved by a Muhammadan *Farras* (bed-servant) named Madari Mehtar. His principal naval officer was a Mussalman named Sidi Misri. He took the help of all and had places for all in his service, irrespective of religion. He did not hate Muslims. On the contrary in order to show equal respect to their religious sentiments, he erected a special Mosque at Raigad in front of his own palace.

8. *Aurangzeb's correct estimate of the danger*

And lastly, the best evidence of Shivaji's aim is supplied by Emperor Aurangzeb himself. Why did such a shrewd and wise Emperor spend the best part of his life and all his imperial resources in the conquest of the Deccan ? One cannot say that he was acting thoughtlessly or in a chimerical fashion. Aurangzeb clearly saw the danger to his empire. He well knew Shivaji's aims. He was convinced that Shivaji aimed a blow at the empire itself. That is the reason why, as soon as he learnt that Shivaji was dead and that his rebel son Akbar in conjunction with Sambhaji had formed dangerous designs against his own power, he came down to give a death-blow to this delayed project once for all. That it proved futile is a different matter. But that wise Emperor's policy clearly proves the aims which Shivaji had formed, and which his successors persistently tried to accomplish long after his death.

9. *The War of Independence*

I need not detain you long over the period that lies between the deaths of the two great creators of Maratha history, I mean, Shivaji and Aurangzeb. This period, while it has on the one hand shed the brightest lustre on the Maratha name, has also, on the other hand, given rise to that pernicious system known as the *Saranjami*, which Shivaji had studiously put down and which in the end destroyed the homogeneity of the Maratha nation. Shivaji's death was both sudden and premature. His son Sambhaji, although brave and spirited, was not equal to the task of facing the several enemies attacking him at the same time, the principal among whom was Aurangzeb, who came down like an avalanche upon the Maratha Raj. Although Sambhaji waged a most heroic struggle, he was captured and beheaded with cruel indignity, achieving by his heroic death what he failed to do in his fateful life. These very misfortunes, however, nerved a band of patriots, Brahmans, Marathas and Prabhus, to unite for the common purpose of defending national liberty.

The more famous names among these patriots were Pralhad Niraji, Ramchandra Pant Amatya, Parashuram Trimbak Pratinidhi, Dhanaji Jadhav, Senapati Santaji Ghorpade, Khando Ballal Chitnis, Shankraji Narayan Sachiv and others, presided over by the genial king Rajaram, the younger son of Shivaji. Although working under great disadvantages, these patriots carried on the long war against Aurangzeb to a successful issue. The powerful Emperor was so discomfited that he had to find in death a final release from all his troubles and misfortunes. Writes Ranade : " Without revenues, without armies, without forts and without resources of any kind, the Maratha leaders managed to raise armies, retake forts, and develop a system of conquest by which they regained not only the swarajya but also the right to levy Chauthai and Sardeshmukhi. Many of these patriots who conceived and carried out this plan of operations, died in the midst of the struggle, but their places were taken up by others with equal devotion and success. The credit of all this must be ascribed to Aurangzeb's ambition. He stirred the people of Maharastra to their utmost depths and it was the hard discipline of this twenty years' war which cemented the national and political instincts of their leaders and during the next three generations carried them as conquerors to the farthest parts of India. It was a higher moral force which brought out all the virtues of the best men of the nation, heroism, noble endurance, administrative skill, hope which rose higher with every disappointment, a sense of brotherhood in common danger, a trust in the final success of their cause, because it was the cause of their religion. Hence this war of independence is regarded as constituting the most eventful period of Maratha history."

10. *How Shivaji's example inspired others*

We can now easily conceive, how at a time of intense depression, the Marathas were able to fire the imagination of all the martial races of India, to whom the example of Shivaji and his followers imparted not only the Maratha spirit and enthusiasm, but also their hope and patriotism, and a practical lesson in warfare and independence, which soon became so catching, that they steeled the hearts of the Sikhs, the Jats, the Rajputs and the Bundelas who all seized the opportunity for a national rising after the death of Aurangzeb. I shall now try to offer a few remarks in order to explain Shivaji's conception of the Maratha constitution.

We know that from small beginnings Shivaji laid the foundation of the Maratha Kingdom, the exact constitution of which has been variously interpreted. Some liken his constitution of the eight ministers to the present day cabinets ; but these eight ministers had no independant powers, and Shivaji cannot be said to have made an arrangement involving on his part the surrender of any bit of his authority in favour of any of his ministers. Shivaji was an autocrat, a benevolent despot, however wisely he may have ruled his kingdom. His will was law, although he directed it to the best interests of his nation. As a rule, we eastern peoples are swayed, in all our concerns, political, social or any other, by entirely individual influences. We have never been amenable to the discipline required for the healthy conduct of constitutional bodies. Even the word 'constitution' is foreign to us. Particularly has this been the case with the Marathas. If we are fortunate enough to have a wise chief to direct our destinies, our affairs look bright and prosperous : if we happen to get a bad ruler or a nonentity at our head, decline. "If good, so much the better ; if evil, tyrannical and oppressive, they must needs submit and wait until the tyranny was overpassed." So long as Shivaji was living, the whole nation supported and obeyed him ; the moment he was gone and affairs fell into the hands of his degenerate son, the whole nation was at his mercy for weal or woe. His second son Rajaram, in later days, allowed full scope to his ministers and generals, who, having been trained under Shivaji, possessed exceptional capacity which enabled the nation to wage a successful war with the most tenacious of the Mughal Emperors. Things took an altogether different turn at the return of Shahu after Aurangzeb's death, and constituted, what we can call a complete transformation in Maratha polity from its original plan which it is my purpose now to explain.

11. *Chauthai, its origin and purpose.*

One very useful instrument of a political character, which Shivaji wisely forged and himself brought into practice, was his system of levying impositions on an enemy country known as *Chauthai* and *Sardeshmukhi*, the former being of the nature of a tribute exacted from hostile or conquered territories, and the latter a kind of revenue ownership, that is, *Watan* as they called it, which the leaders of the Maratha bands claimed as their own in the old Bahamani days, and which they never ceased to exact in later times. The practice of exacting Chauth, *i.e.* one-fourth of the estimated revenue, is supposed, on fresh evidence recently published, to have existed in the western parts of India long before the days of Shivaji. Prof. Pissurlencar of Goa, and Dr. Surendra Nath Sen of Calcutta, after examining the Portuguese archives there, have published papers dating 1595, 1604-1606, 1634, showing that the Raja of Ramnagar in north Konkan exacted this Chauth from the Portuguese possession of Daman, on the ground that those territories used to pay the Chauth to the kings of Ramnagar, before they passed into the hands of the Portuguese.[1] The practice was quickly taken up by Shivaji and was applied by him to the territories and principalities, which he overran or subjugated, guaranteeing, in return for the payment, immunity from any more exactions on his own part, and security from molestation by any other power. This practice of levying Chauth on foreign territories either fully or partially conquered or often merely overrun, proved a ready instrument in the hands of Shivaji's successors and enabled them to expand their power to the distant quarters of India. During the critical and confused times that followed the capture of Sambhaji by Aurangzeb, this

*Set Dr. Sen's *Military System of the Marathas* wherein the subject has been fully treated.

practice of levying Chauth proved a useful measure to the various leaders of roving Maratha bands, and enabled them to resist the Emperor successfully. It is in this measure, coupled with the system of guerilla tactics, that we can trace the subtle influence of the Maratha power, which began slowly to eat into the vitals of the Mughal Empire. It will be worth our while to look a little more closely into the subject, and fully grasp the various factors existing in the situation of Maharastra, in order to understand the changes in the Maratha constitution, that took place later on, that is, during the latter days of Aurangzeb's invasion and at the time of his death.

12. *Love of the Maratha Deshmukhs for their patrimony*

The Marathas have been described as by nature very jealous of their *Watans* or lands inherited from ancestors, for which they had often paid dearly even with their lives. When during the Bahamani rule or perhaps even earlier, the country of Maharastra was settled and brought under cultivation, the inducement offered to the various Maratha families was the grant of *Watan* lands in perpetuity. The hilly sloping country of the Western Ghats. known in history as the Mavals, or the land of the setting sun, was first cleared of forests and wild animals, and made habitable by several immigrant Kshatriyas now known by the common appellation of the Mavalas, whom later Shivaji subdued and turned into helpmates, mainly by stratagem and occasionally by the sword, but who in the beginning acted as small independent rulers of the tracts which they owned as Deshmukhs, meaning heads of the *Desh*, or feudal landlords as we can style them. The Moreys, the Shirkes, the Dalvis, the Jedhes, the Jadhavs, the Nimbalkars, the Khopdes and others, who all figure so prominently in the early activites of Shivaji, were hereditary Deshmukhs or Watandars, whose duty it was to colonize and settle and populate the country, so as to make it yield revenue to Government. The process was long and troublesome, involved a tremendous cost of life, labour and money, and naturally created intense love and interest in the owners' mind for the land which they served and improved from generation to generation. The Government of the country granted these Maratha adventurers periodical leases and immunity from taxation. When the lands came to be finally improved and became capable of yielding an annual revenue, the work of collection was entrusted to these same Deshmukhs, who were asked to pay 90% of the estimated revenue to Government, keeping for themselves the remaining 10% as a reward for their labours. This share of 10% came to be called Sardeshmukhi and was, in essence and origin, a constant source of hereditary income, which all Maratha sardars from the Chhatrapati down to the smallest holder claimed as their ancestral patrimony, and which they most jealously guarded and preserved, even at the risk of life. Readers of Maratha history may remember how Chhatrapati Shahu strictly and rigidly reserved for himself this 10% charge of the Sardeshmukhi dues, when his Peshwa Balaji Vishvanath obtained from the Sayyads, imperial sanads of Chauth and Sardeshmukhi in the year 1718, and how he distributed the proceeds of the latter among his various favourites and the persons who had helped him in his difficulties. The Bhosles themselves were originally Sardeshmukhs on a par with the Jadhavs and Moreys, although they succeeded in establishing an independent Maratha kingdom later on. This nature of Sardeshmukhi deserves to be clearly noted as distinct from that of the Chauth, a different item altogether, which was mainly designed for subjugating foreign territory, and which had the nature of a tribute.

The Maratha Deshmukhs had thus vested interests in the lands of the Deccan for centuries before the rise of Shivaji, and were practically independent of the ruling authorities, who could chastise them only if they failed to pay the Government revenue. The precarious and adventurous life which for a long time they led in the Maval lands, has been reflected in the plentiful old papers, which have been lately discovered and published, mainly by Rajwade in those of his volumes, which deal with the Shivaji period, *i.e.*, 15 to 18, 20 and 22. Disputes about rights and possession, about heirs and succession, about thefts and robberies, murder and molestations of various kinds, which were so numerous and acute for about a century before the rise of Shivaji and which have been fully described in those papers, supply a clear idea about the state of the country at the time and the manner in which Shivaji utilized them to his own advantage. Shivaji, shrewd as he was in estimating the inherent capacity of these Mavalas, found in them ready material for his nation-building activities. The strength and energy of these Maval Deshmukhs, were till then being entirely wasted in internecine disputes and family feuds, making murder, arson, waylaying and other crimes, matters of common occurrence, which the distant rulers of Bijapür and Ahmadnagar could hardly check or stop, owing to the difficult and impassable nature of the country and the turbulent spirit of the people. In fact, Shivaji's father Shahji had already enlisted the sympathies of some of these Maval Deshmukhs, in his wars against the onrushing Mughals, leaving the completion of his task to his astute son Shivaji. The Jedhes and the Bandals who were in Shahji's employ, continued to help his son Shivaji, when he started his national work in Maharastra, and after his father had transferred his own field of activity to the distant south. Of the Maval Deshmukhs the Moreys happened to be by far the most powerful and influential in the service of Bijapur, and having resisted the early activities of Shivaji, came into direct conflict with him and brought upon themselves severe chastisement at his hands. In accounting for the rapid and phenomenal success of Shivaji, we must take note of this turbulent spirit of the Maval Deshmukhs and their intense love for their original patrimony. In the latter days of Maratha rule, we often notice how the Sindias of Gwalior, the Pawars of Dhar, or the Gaikwads of Baroda, Jealously guarded their small hereditary Watans or Deshmukhis in the Deccan, even when they had created extensive kingdoms for themselves outside in Malwa and Gujarat. The *Saranjami* system introduced by the Peshwas, it will be seen later, is based on this love of the Marathas for their hereditary lands in the Deccan.

13, *Origin of Sardeshmukhi and Saranjami.*

To understand the real nature of Sardeshmukhi, we must study the structure and practices of the village government obtaining in Maharastra from the profuse materials which have been published in the form of the legal decisions on the disputes of those times. The *Watan* claims have been of various kinds. The *Patel* or *Patil* is the headman of the village, looking after all its concerns, and the *Kulkarni* is his writer who keeps the village records. The Patel and the Kulkarni used to have land assignments for their services, *i.e.*, also *Watans* in a certain sense. Patvaris and Pandes, Goudas and Nadgoudas are merely provincial synonyms of the Patel and the Kulkarni, the first two being used in the Central Provinces, and the last two in the Kanarese country in the south. *Desai* is the corruption of the Sanskrit term *Desha-swami*, or possibly *Deshapati*, also styled Deshmukh. The *Sardeshmukh* stands above several Desais or Deshmukhs, *i.e.*, looks after a group of several villages. *Saranjam* in later times came to mean land assignment given for military service : the word *Saranjam*, which means provision, occurs in the papers of Shivaji's time. When a title or a mark of honour, such as a horse, an elephant, or a palanquin was bestowed by the king upon his deserving servants or subjects, it was supposed to carry with it a provision for its maintenance. *viz.*, the *Saranjam*. In later times, however, this word came to mean provision for military service only, for employing and maintaining troops to fight the battles of Government ; those holding landed Saranjams of this nature are styled Saranjamdars, who date their rise particularly from the times of Shivaji's son Rajaram and who were chiefly instrumental in the later expansion of the Maratha power at the hands of the Peshwas. In popular language the words Saranjam and

Jagir mean nearly the same thing. The present Rajas and Maharajas such as those of Gwalior, Indore, Baroda, Dhar, Dewas in Central India, or of Miraj, Sangli, Jamkhindi and Ramdurg in the south, were all Saranjamdars of a certain type, with definite rules and regulations about their service, which we find amply illustrated in the *Peshwa's Diaries* printed from the Poona Daftar particularly in the volumes referring to Madhav Rao I. As this system of Saranjamdars with many fresh Maratha capitals from which their rule radiated, has come to be known as the particular creation of the Peshwas and has often been held more or less responsible for the fall of the Marathas, it is necessary to understand its exact origin and nature in the constitution of the Maratha kingdom. As the subject is complicated and not properly grasped by the average student, I have purposely tried to explain it at such length.

Shivaji was deadly against assigning lands in perpetuity for any purpose whatsoever, and stopped the old practice with a firm hand, often confiscating all lands and jagirs which had been made over to generals during preceding regimes, and substituting cash payment for them. Rajwade's volumes dealing with the Shivaji period are full of papers which show how Shivaji laid his hand on all lands which had been given away. He clearly realized the disadvantages of the system of creating feudal lords. In those days of unrest and confusion, it was difficult, particularly on account of the absence of good roads and means of communication, to exercise strict control over military leaders enjoying feudal jagirs. They often rebelled against authority, openly joined the enemy, invariably neglected to keep efficient troops for service, and tried to accumulate money and power at the expense of the State, more or less after the fashion of feudalism in Europe. Although of course the allurement of landed jagirs succeeded for a time in securing conspicuous service and daring from soldiers and their leaders, their successors were not necessarily as brave, willing and faithful, in their service and claimed to enjoy their patrimony without giving an adequate return to the State. One who acquired a jagir for the first time, must have been a fit person deserving the reward for the service and sacrifice which he had rendered to the State ; but his successors usually proved quite unfit ; if they were dispossessed of their holdings, they became disaffected and troublesome to the State in a hundred ways. Shivaji very early in his career fully realized the disadvantages of the system, and paid all kinds of service in ready cash, with which he was ever careful to keep himself well supplied. He even confiscated lands given to various religious institutions or charities, and substituted cash payment for them.

But this wise policy had to be discontinued after Shivaji's death, owing to a combination of adverse circumstances to which I must now refer. The powerful Emperor Aurangzeb descended upon Maharastra in 1683, with a huge and well-quipped army, determined to complete the task of subjugating the Deccan, begun by his three illustrious predecessors, and put into the field the vast resources of his extensive empire to attain his object. The very names of the generals who served under him, would have struck terror into any people he proposed to conquer. In a short time he annexed the two kingdoms of Bijapur and Golconda, captured and killed the Maratha King Sambhaji, taking into captivity his wife and son, and nearly accomplishing his grand purpose with one stroke. It was in the midst of such a depressing situation, that Shivaji's second son Rajaram started his work of saving his nation, by catching at any and every means that came ready to his hand, working also the system of Chauthai for extending the Maratha power. How he obtained adherence to his cause, can be well understood from the following typical letter written by Rajaram in July 1696 to Sadashiv Naik, the ruler of Sunda, a small State to the south-east of Goa. The letter was written from Jinji, when the Emperor was threatening to conquer not only the Marathas, but also other more or less independent States and territories throughout south India. Thus runs the letter : " We are glad to have received your letter and the messages which you sent with your two trusted agents Konherpant and Rayaji Rukmangad, who have communicated and explained to us all the details of the negotiation in connection with your offer of mutual help and perpetual friendship in our present situation. We have considered the proposal fully in conference with our ministers Shankaraji Pandit Sumant and Nilo Krishna, and are glad, as requested by you, to commit this agreement to writing, and send it on to you with our solemn oath for its observance on our part, and trust you will do the same on yours.

"Your proposal was that the territory of the Panch-Mahals with all its forts and places, should be assigned to you and your successors in perpetuity in return for a yearly tribute of 22,200 Hons (Rs. 78,000), an amount which you are at present paying to Muhammadan rulers. We accept this proposal, undertake to vanquish the Muhammadans and protect you from them or from any other enemies that will molest you. When your enemies will be so vanquished, you must regularly pay the amount of tribute to us from year to year. Moreover, you must also carry on an aggressive war with the Muhammadans, and we vouchsafe to you the fresh territory you will be able to conquer from the enemy on payment by you to us, of the customary tributes assigned to those territories, in recognition of our suzerain power. Whenever you would be threatened or molested by any outsider, our forces shall at once run to your help and win peace and safety for you. Thus shall we continue ever to remain friendly with your State, and in token of our solemn promise to that effect we send you separately *bilva* leaves and flower garlands of Mahadeva and bread. We trust you will accept these and continue to increase the solemn friendship ever hereafter."*

When Rajaram retired from Maharastra to Jinji, there was no money in his treasury. Raigad, the capital of the Maratha kingdom, was in the hands of the Emperor. There were no Maratha army and no government. It was only the undaunted brains of a few clever supporters of Rajaram, warriors and statesmen, that rose to the

**Shiva Charitra Sahitya III.* 482

occasion and invented means and appliances in order to save the situation as best they could. The Emperor, on the other hand, kept a full watch over the measures and activities of his opponents and did his best to seduce the Maratha fighters, by offering them all possible inducements to join his army and fight the fugitive Chhatrapati. He granted Inams and jagirs to those Maratha leaders who had been persecuted by Sambhaji and thereby managed to weaken the Maratha cause immensely. In these adverse circumstances Rajaram and his advisers were compelled to offer, on their part also, the same inducements to their helpers, in order to retain their services and allegiance. I might here give a sample of what Rajaram wrote to the Maratha leaders : "We note with pleasure that you have preserved the country and served the King loyally. You are highly brave and serviceable. We know that you hold Inam lands from the Emperor, but that you are now ready to forsake him and fight for us and suffer hardships for us and our nation. The Emperor has created a havoc in the land. He has converted the Hindus wholesale to his creed. Therefore, you should cautiously conduct measures of safety and retaliation and keep us duly informed of your services. If you do not swerve from loyalty and if you help the State in its present sore extremity, we solemnly bind ourselves to continue your hereditary holdings to you and your heirs and successors."

In this way, letters and sanads granting Inams and jagirs began to pour from the Maratha Court in an unbroken current. The main purport of them was, that the Maratha bands should roam anywhere and everywhere, plunder the imperial treasure and territory and harass the enemy in all possible ways. These sanads were nothing but promises of future reward, assuring the military leaders that they would be considered owners of the territory they would subjugate in any quarter of India. This game became profitable for a time to the roving Maratha bands; they borrowed money, raised troops and carried on expeditions to distant parts. The process gave a sudden impetus to the business of banking and fighting. Let me quote only one instance.

Ramchandra Pant, the great Amatya of Rajaram, recommends to his master the services of one Patankar in a letter which runs thus : "These Patankars own hereditary *Watans*. They have undertaken to raise 5,000 troops and will be styled Pancha-sahasri. This kingdom belongs to gods, Marathas and Brahmans ; the Patankars have undergone terrible hardships in crushing the armies of the enemy. In this task they have not only spent all they had, but also contracted huge debts. Therefore, their sacrifices deserve to be adequately rewarded, and so we shall allow them the following 12 villages in perpetual *Inam.*" Requests for similar *Inams* and rewards began to pour in thousands before the Maratha administrators of the day. They particularly bring their fivefold service to the notice of the Chhatrapati. They say : (1) "We have not joined the Mughals ; (2) we have managed to carry on cultivation ; (3) we pay revenue to Government ; (4) we have employed large forces to protect the country from robbers and raiders, and, in addition (5) we fight the battles of the Chhatrapati at the risk of our lives." This is not all. They also repeat the inducements that the Emperor had offered them, and demand something better from their own master, saying in effect, "We, your own kith and kin, should not at least fare worse than those who go and obtain handsome rewards from him." We thus clearly see how the system of Jagirs and military *Saranjams,* so sternly put down by Shivaji, came to be revived once more, and how it took deep root during the long and confused period of the Emperor's campaigns in the Deccan. In fact the confusion created by the numerous indiscriminate grants of Inam was so great, that Rajaram on his return from Jinji to Satara, found that one and the same district was claimed by several persons at one time, and he had therefore to appoint a special court of enquiry to adjust all claims of land *Watans,* and revoke or confirm them on certain fixed principles. When Rajaram died in 1700, and his queen Tara Bai managed the Government for the next few years, she tried her best to stop the practice of granting new *Saranjams,* and even to cancel some of those that had been already given. She and her advisers were fully aware how the departure from the healthy regulations of Shivaji was leading the kingdom towards ultimate ruin, but were unable, under the stress of circumstances and for mere self-protection, to stop the practice, which by prescription had become hardened for years.

14. *Perversion of the original object.*

It soon became very difficult for the central Government to keep these jagirdars in proper check and exact discipline and service from them. They even alienated their own Inam lands within their sphere, to whomsoever they pleased. I give a sample here of the sanads issued by the Chhatrapati in answer to the clamorous petitions that poured constantly for *Inams* : they run thus :—

"At such and such a place you came to His Highness the Chhatrapati with a request that your ancestors had been serving the State in succession for a long time. That you yourself also wish to serve loyally and faithfully ever hereafter ; that you have a large family, and that His Highness should out of kindness provide for its maintenance. Taking this request of yours into kind consideration, His Highness has been pleased to grant such and such a village as *Inam* in perpetuity to you, your heirs and successors. We enjoin on all our successors, on oath, that this Inam should not be taken back." Such requests evidently mean that what was granted first for hazardous and faithful service, was claimed by the successors for mere maintenance and enjoyment of a large family of idlers, who rendered no service to Government and claimed gratuitous reward. This habit of enjoying land assignments without personal fitness and without giving any labour in return, sapped the very foundations of public service and even the morals of society itself. The Brahmans continued to extract any sum from one rupee to a lac and more from Government, which had assumed the pleasing role of protecting Brahmans and cows, for no other visible service than the questionable one of performing religious rites and showering blessings upon the King and the State and praying for their success and well-being.

It was beggary of the very worst type, giving prominence to birth, heredity and prescriptive rights, leaving no room to Government for the recognition of fresh merit and individual capacity. All the Maratha State came to be alienated in this way. Those who served and sacrificed themselves, and those who did not, came to be put on the same level. This was the greatest defect of the *Saranjami* system, which in no small degree contributed to the ruin of the structure so cleverly raised by Shivaji.

It is also interesting to trace how all these defects came to be perpetuated under the conditions that then prevailed. During the confusion and weakness that overtook the Mughal Empire after Aurangzeb's death, many proud and ambitious Maratha leaders roamed about the country, and took possession of whatever territories they could lay their hands on ; but this conquest was by no means homogeneous like the Raj of Shivaji, which he had conquered by means of armies paid by himself and directly controlled by him. The various Maratha leaders of the later days, were not subject to the control of one single power and were scattered units having no cohesion. The astute Amatya Ramchandra Pant tried to control them to some extent, but they often proved recalcitrant, looking to their own selfish interests and being ever ready to join the enemy, if better prospects were offered them. If Ramchndra Pant had tried to exact stricter discipline from them, they would in all probability have openly accepted the Mughal service. Owing to these difficulties the Marathas could not gradually build up a solid constitution by degrees, such as the British did in their own country.

It must, however, be borne in mind that such a comparison is often pointless, as we have not before us all the facts of the situation. Many problems of history can be rightly solved, if we have a proper conception of the surroundings and circumstances affecting them. We can know very well, why the Government founded by Shivaji did not last long after him and how the system built up by the Peshwas differed entirely from Shivaji's original conception. So, no hard and fast constitution could in those days be thought of, when there were many disturbing elements facing the workers on all sides.

One reason why the system of creating jagirs or military cantonments at different places all over the country, became absolutely necessary during the Peshwas' days, was that there were no military roads for rapid communication and movement of armies, from the central seat of Government to any threatened point. During Shivaji's days the central Mughal Government was powerful and he dared not cross the Narmada for any ambitious project beyond ; Shivaji had to remain satisfied with whatever he could achieve in Maharastra proper and in the farthest south. But after Aurangzeb's death, there was a general scramble for conquest and power, in which even the western nations began to take a part. If the Peshwas had confined their efforts to the south only, the Rajputs and provincial governors and local chiefs of the north would, in all probability, have established independent rulerships, which it would have cost the Peshwas more effort and expense to conquer, when they attempted to accomplish the ideal of *Hindu-pad-Padshahi*. So, having realized that the time was opportune for carrying out that ideal, upon the death of Aurangzeb, the leaders assembled and took counsel together at the Court of Shahu, and with his permission, formed plans of conquest, divided the spheres of activity between the various workers and started on their mission, with no clear cut plan or regulations to guide or bind them together. The idea was to choose a centre for military control, and establish there permanent Maratha settlements, with strong family interests, a method by which the country soon became dotted with small Maratha capitals, each with a wall or fortification and having a sufficient establishment for military and revenue purposes. In its original conception and outline, the system had no inherent defects ; and had there been provision for sufficient check from the central Government and no tendency to insubordination on the part of the executors, it would have worked well ; in fact it did work satisfactorily so long as the controlling authority at the capital was strong, and so long as there was no competition with European Powers of superior organization and armament.

Thus, the *Saranjami* system supplied the want of good military roads from Satara and Poona to the various centres outside, which it was not possible for the Peshwas to build in a short time and with the scanty resources which they possessed. Even before the leaders started on an expedition, or what is called *muluk-giri* in technical language, they tried to obtain *sanads* for jagirs in the territories which they proposed to invade.* The advent of Shahu did not improve matters. The Peshwas did try to reduce to obedience the older ministers and leaders of Shivaji's days ; but in order to accomplish this, they had to create new sardars of their own, like the Sindias and the Holkars, who later imitated their predecessors and in their own turn resented control from the weaker Peshwas. If the Peshwas had attempted to enforce stricter discipline, they would not have succeeded in accomplishing even what they did. In fact, the India of the 18th century, with the weakening of the central Mughal Government, afforded a particularly favourable field to very many ambitious and roving spirits. The provincial governors of the Emperors, such as Safdar Jang, Alivardi Khan, Nizam-ul-Mulk, the various Bundela princes and Sikh generals, Jat and Rohilla chiefs in the north, the Nawabs of Arcot, Savanur, Kadappa, Karnool, and the more or less powerful rulers of Mysore, Bednor and other places in the south,—all these tried, each in his own way, to obtain independent power and submitted to superior strength only for the time when they were compelled. The Maratha armies often reduced them to obedience, but the moment the armies left their frontiers, they once more resumed their previous activities. Year after year, the Peshwa had to send military expeditions all over India to collect tribute : thus it has to be admitted that the *Hindu-pad-Padshahi* which the Peshwas attempted to establish, was more a resounding name than an actually accomplished fact.

* See *S. C. Sahitya* V. 767

LECTURE IV

SHAHU AND THE MARATHA EXPANSION

1. *Early life of Shahu,—situation at Aurangzeb's death.*

Having taken a review of the conditions under which the Maratha kingdom had its start, and of the development of the *Saranjami* system, during the perilous days of Sambhaji and Rajaram, we shall now turn our attention to the next phase of Maratha polity, which has reference to the changes that took place in the situation of Maharastra in consequence of the death of Aurangzeb. This situation contains some salient features which do not seem to have been properly grasped by students of Mahatha history, and which alone will enable them to form a proper estimate of the policy and achievements of the Peshwas. The first and foremost point that deserves to be noted in this connection is, the nature and character of Shahu's personality, which not only influenced and controlled Maratha politics during his ease-loving reign of nearly half a century, but gave a definite shape to the future course of the Maratha kingdom.

Next to the great founder Shivaji, Shahu has played the most important part in the development of the Maratha State. Shahu, born in May 1682, roamed about as a child with his circumspect mother Yesubai and his dashing father Sambhaji, undergoing exceptional privations and troubles, which came to an end when he was captured at the age of seven by Aurangzeb at the fall of Raigad, and kept in secure custody in the moving imperial camp, where all personal comforts were provided for him, by the kindly attentions of Aurangzeb's daughter Zinatun-nisa Begam. Aurangzeb himself, foiled in his endeavour to crush the Maratha power by his cruel treatment of their king and shrewdly concealing his evil intentions for this harmless son of his dead enemy, brought him up in his own camp, with a view to using him as a pawn in his game of vanquishing the Marathas as circumstances would require. Having spent in captivity 18 long years, that is the best part of his youth or the period for learning and study, and having been brought up in the imperial zenana, Shahu developed an altogether soft and effeminate character, although he never lost his innate love and warmth of heart towards his own people ; he also possessed enough common sense, practical wisdom in judging men and matters, and above all an intensely obliging and generous nature. He was always afraid of committing sin or doing wrong. His great and only drawback was his love of ease, and an aversion for active military life by leading soldiers on a battle-field. He thus remained always ignorant of even the geography of the various places where his ministers and commanders were executing his plans and orders. Aurangzeb had always used him as a weapon in the game of war he was playing against the Marathas. He in vain tried to convert him to the Muslim faith, and even offered to allow him to go from his camp under surveillance and to rule as a vassal to the Mughals. But Shahu refused to take advantage of this half-hearted prospect of release, suspecting sinister motives on the part of the Emperor, after whose death he followed Azam Shah's march to the north and left the Mughal camp near Bhopal, returning to the Deccan to win the Maratha Kingdom from his aunt Tarabai, a design long contrived by the aged Emperor of creating a division in the Maratha ranks. He had to dispute the Maratha throne with his cousin Shivaji and his astute aunt Tarabai. Shahu's mother, wives, and cousins were taken to Delhi as hostages, lest he should throw away his allegiance to the Emperor and declare his independence. In fact, it was upon his stipulating always to remain a loyal vassal to Delhi and obey the orders of the Emperor in his hour of need, that he was released and allowed to go back to his country from beyond the Narmada.

Possessing a God-fearing and pious nature, Shahu faithfully observed his promise, and ever after strongly resisted all temptations or solicitations from his advisers to declare open hostility against the imperial authority. His grandfather Shivaji started his life's work in declared opposition to Muslim rule, by the suppression of which he hoped to establish an independent kingdom of his own. Shahu, on the other hand, altogether renounced this avowed principle, even forgot the terrible war which his father and uncle had waged with the Emperor for a quarter of a century, and ordered his generals and ministers to carve out new spheres of influence and activity, without damaging the central Mughal authority. This impossible task was thrown on the shoulders of Shahu's Peshwas, who did their best, on the one hand, to keep Shahu at ease, and on the other, to carry out the work of the *Hindu-Pad-Padshahi*, as best they could, trying to accomplish the ideal of Shivaji, as much as possible, in the altered conditions of their position. In fact the very first expedition of Peshwa Balaji Visvanath to Delhi in 1718, was undertaken at the express desire of Shahu to help the Emperor Farrukhsiyar out of his wretched situation. This dubious position of the Peshwa must ever be kept in view, in order to understand the oft-questioned anomaly, why the Nizam was allowed to remain a constant and dangerous neighbour, and why he was not finally conquered or crushed by the Peshwas in the south. It is indeed a curious phenomenon that when the Peshwas' troops were making distant conquests of Attock and Mysore, places nearer home like Ahmadnagar, Trimbak and Junnar remained Muhammadan possessions. In recent political parlance, Shahu with his God-fearing kindly disposition can be rightly styled the author of non-violence, on the strength of which the Maratha Kingdom rapidly developed in extent and power. His death so reversed this policy that a strong opposition arose from the Muslims of north India, culminating in the disaster of Panipat.

2. *Division of the Maratha Kingdom,—why the Peshwas looked to the north*

How wisely Shahu managed to put a stop to the civil war which, by his release, the Emperor expected to start in the Deccan, in order thereby to crush the rising Marathas indirectly, may be gathered from the way in which Shahu, immediately after his coronation in January 1708, offered his cousin Shivaji a half share of the kingdom as it then existed, although Tarabai claimed the whole of it. The situation of Shahu in the Deccan for the first four or five years after his release, was extremely precarious. Tarabai declared him an impostor, alleging that the kingdom which the great Shivaji had founded, had been lost by his son Sambhaji, that Rajaram, her husband, had created it entirely anew, that therefore it legally belonged to her son only, and that Shahu had no claim to it. Shahu, however, showed phenomenal activity in his first struggle with his aunt and cousin, which lasted some four years, at the end of which she and her son were taken prisoners by Sambhaji, the second son of Rajaram, with whom Shahu later on entered into a treaty of peace. He formed two divisions of the kingdom ; that to the south of the river Krishna he made over to Sambhaji, taking himself the one to the north of that river. The whole Maratha kingdom at the time hardly extended beyond the two modern districts of Satara and Poona, and although having divided it into halves Shahu came to possess quite an insignificant area, he secured, by the above mentioned arrangement, full liberty to acquire a fresh field for expansion in the north, as the south was closed to him, having been handed over to his cousin. This point must be clearly borne in mind by those, who are disposed to find fault with Shahu for having undertaken costly distant expeditions in the north, before setting in order his own house in the Deccan. The famous controversy between Shahu's Pratinidhi and his Peshwa Baji Rao I., which has been graphically described by Grant Duff and others, and which is probably a myth, centres round this division of the Maratha kingdom, and shows how Shahu had no choice in the matter. He had either to remain contented with his small patrimony in the midst of warring elements, without hope of ever extending his dominion, or forcibly to create a new kingdom in the north.

When the division was effected, it was understood, we may be sure, that both Sambhaji and Shahu were to work zealously in their respective spheres ; but Sambhaji wasted away his resources and opportunity, his time and energy, in useless family squabbles and vain intrigues to put down Shahu, while Shahu employed in his service such active and vigorous men as Peshwa Baji Rao, Senapati Dabhade, Sindia, Udaji Pawar, Kanhoji and Raghuji Bhosle, Malharrao Holkar, Babuji Naik, the Barves, the Joshis of Chas, the Hingnes, the Bokils and others, giving free scope to their valour and statesmanship. An empire, like a personal estate, goes on gradually expanding at the hands of shrewd managers ; if the overgrown Maratha empire fell at last, it cannot be due to the fault of Shahu in having built and expanded it : and no amount of care in setting the house in order at the beginning, could have averted its ultimate fate, as we know it now.

Malwa has been the key to Indian supremacy as much in modern as in ancient days. How essential a foothold in Malwa is to the aspirants for domination over this vast continent is lucidly and ably enunciated by the learned author of "Malwa in Transition"; and I would advise my readers to study carefully chapter III of that recent publication. Writes the author—" The control of the six subahs of the Deccan meant the acquisition of a great power. But to control the Deccan necessitated some domination over Malwa which alone commanded the route between the north and the south. The prosperity of Malwa too made it important. Thus for reasons political and financial the various nobles at the Court struggled for the control of Malwa." Jaisinh had his own leanings towards the Marathas, and the latter's advent into Malwa brought them together again. Moreover the period saw the beginning of a new policy for the Mughal Empire. First its officers, and later the Emperor himself began to offer terms to the Marathas, who threatened to dominate the scene in the coming decade. Balaji Vishvanath strengthened the position of Shahu and planned an aggressive policy. Shahu himself advocated co-operation with the imperial authorities. He declared, "I have given a sacred promise to the Emperor Aurangzeb that I would render all possible help to the Empire if it came to be threatened by a foreign enemy : that I would do all I can to protect it."* These extraneous circumstances are often lost sight of by students of the subject in accounting for the Maratha advance towards the north.

3. *Services of Balaji Vishvanath*

A third feature of the situation in the Deccan deserves to be mentioned now. As I have said before, when Shahu came back from the Emperor's camp and reached Satara towards the end of 1707, his fortune was at the lowest ebb. Most of the powerful Maratha leaders had espoused the cause of Tarabai, who stoutly opposed the claims of Shahu. Senapati Dhanaji Jadhav alone went over to Shahu, but his death soon after weakened Shahu's cause again, and the mischief was made worse by the defection of Dhanaji's son Chandrasen Jadhav. Faced with this treachery, Shahu would not have been able to maintain his position but for the timely and loyal help of Balaji Vishvanath. He therefore rewarded Balaji's services with the Peshwaship to which he was appointed in the year 1713. Balaji's first concern was threefold ; *viz.*, to strengthen the cause of Shahu by bringing over to his side, as many powerful sardars and sympathisers of Tarabai as possible, to create order and peace in the, few territories which Shahu then owned, and to give useful employment to the various turbulent Maratha bands who, being flushed with their

* P. D. S. 30·222

recent victory over the imperial forces, would simply have ruined the nation for want of a suitable occupation, by taking sides in the civil war which had not yet ended. The services and achievements of this first Peshwa have not yet received proper recognition in history, since they are matters of only recent research. Shahu in one of his letters styles him *atula-parakrami-sevaka, i.e.,* " a servant of incomparable capacity," showing thereby that Shahu did not bestow his Peshwaship on a mere clerk in the employ of the Senapati, but on a worthy person of proved merit, after a full trial of 5 years and a close personal acquaintance going back to a much longer period. In fact, although sufficient details of this first Peshwa's life and work have not yet been discovered, we have enough grounds for asserting that his father and grandfather had been in Shivaji's service, that he possessed long and varied experience obtained by him during the Mughal-Maratha struggle, and consequently a singular grasp of the circumstances and the situation in which Shahu and the whole Maratha nation came to be placed upon the death of Aurangzeb. He also evinced rare foresight and statesmanship in utilizing all available resources towards completing the task of constructing a Hindu empire, which the great Shivaji had set before himself, and which had all but crumbled away during the troubles of the two preceding reigns. Balaji had to look to the north, as his path to the south was permanently closed by the independent existence of Tarabai's kingdom. Balaji found plenty of fighting material scattered all over the country. Several leaders of Maratha bands had long since been making more or less successful incursions into such distant parts as Malwa, Gujarat and Berar. They had ambition and capacity and only needed a field for their activities and a chief to direct them. To check their ambitious spirit was out of the question. The central authority wielded by Shahu was itself weaker than any of these Maratha leaders,—as for instance, Kanhoji Angre of Colaba, Kanhoji Bhosle, Khanderao Dabhade or

* B. I. S. Mandal Quarterly Dec. 1948.

Chandrasen Jadhav, were each singly more than a match for the weak Shahu. The only remedy was to utilize the valiant fighting material for a common purpose and give it a coherent shape, *i.e.*, to create a field in which all could work out their own destiny, by extending Maratha power and influence according to the means and capacity which each possessed. When therefore an appeal for help came to Shahu from the Sayyad ministers of Farrukhsiyar, Balaji at once grasped it and created a diversion which, although but slightly realized at the time even by the persons who took part in it, offered a singular opportunity for the expansion of Maratha power to the distant quarters of India. Balaji's sons, Baji Rao and Chimnaji, were always associated with him not only in his consultations and undertakings, but also in the hardships and trials, which this bold and extensive plan involved. In order to grasp this point fully we must first know some more features of the situation.

4. *The Rajput pact of non-co-operation with the Emperor, —Shankraji Malhar.*

Students of Indian history are already aware how the death of Aurangzeb precipitated a dismemberment of the great Mughal Empire. We must carefully note what old and new powers were ready at the time to take advantage of the situation as it then existed. For instance, the Sikhs were just coming into prominence. Their persecution by Aurangzeb under Guru Govind Sinh gave their activities a military aspect and henceforth throughout the 18th and the first half of the 19th century, the destiny of the frontier province of the Punjab was more or less bound up with the activities of these brave people, the Sikhs. I need not detail here the ambitious designs of some of the provincial Governors, the Nizam, for instance, in the south or the Nawabs of Bengal and Oudh. The Jats and the Rohillas were also coming in for a share of restless prominence. Of all these disintegrating elements the one most conspicuous seems to have escaped the attention of writers on the period, I mean the attitude adopted by the various Rajput princes towards the suzerain Mughal power.* Tod had described the situation in detail, although for want of proper records not then available or for want of the proper historical spirit which was unknown in his time, the subject has not been fully worked out. Aurangzeb had done everything he could to alienate the sympathies of the Rajput princes, who had once been the pillars of the Mughal State, and who remained quiet waiting for an opportunity to wreak their vengeance as soon as the old Emperor had passed away. In the year 1710 they met in a solemn assemblage on the borders of the Pushkar lake near Ajmere and, in deliberate concert, openly threw off their allegiance to the Mughal Emperor, unitedly vowed to stop the practice of giving their daughters in marriage to the Mughal Royal House, and determined to wage open war against the Emperor, in case the latter would force any one of them to break the agreement which they then formed after full and long deliberation. Although this move on the part of the Rajput princes was throughout the 18th century the direct cause of endless trouble, vexation and ruin to themselves, from which they were ultimately rescued only through the intervention of British arms in the early part of the 19th century, it nevertheless forms, so far as our immediate purpose of analysing the historical development is concerned, an important factor of the political situation in India in the early part of the 18th century.

Shahu had occasion to gauge the depth of this Rajput feeling during his long captivity in the Emperor's camp, where many Rajput princes were present in the imperial service. He had gained the sympathies of some of them, was given a cordial send-off by them on his release in Malwa, and being alive to the recent career of Shivaji, they very probably had deliberated together upon measures of concerted action for Hindu regeneration on the part of

* See *Malwa in Transition*. Chap. III section 4 for further elucidation of their subject.

Shahu in the Deccan and on that of the Rajputs in the north. Savai Jaysinh, the Raja of Jaipur, appears to have taken the lead in this new movement, as he all along continued friendly to Maratha overtures even up to the time of his death in 1743. Events doubtless took place later on, which brought about a complete estrangement between the Marathas and the Rajputs ; but we must particularly bear in mind that during Shahu's life-time, there was an entire agreement and cordiality between the two, and both were moved by the same national and religious aspirations. When therefore the first Peshwa Balaji, and after him his soldier son Bajirao I, began their work of building up a Hindu empire for India, their efforts, it must be borne in mind, were fully supported by the prominent Rajput Princes, and Baji Rao was hailed by them as a saviour of their national interests which had long suffered terrible oppression. At any rate, it is enough for our immediate purpose to note the respectful amity that existed between the Marathas and the Rajputs, when Shahu and his first Peshwa began to shape the future destinies of the rising Maratha power. I am sure that with the increasing research in Indian history, to which scholars like Gaurishankar Ojha and others have contributed, fresh materials from Rajput records will corroborate what Maratha and other records have lately brought to light.

A singular personality is seen acting behind the scene at this time. One Shankraji Malhar, once in the employ of Rajaram, working as his *sachiv* or finance minister at Jinji, had, owing to some disagreement which has not been authentically recorded, turned an ascetic and migrated to Benares where he lived for a pretty long time. Shrewd and clever as he was, he had obtained a clear grasp of the situation, both in the south and in the north ; he was conversant with the men and matters in the camp of Aurangzeb as well as with the surroundings of Shahu ; and even when he lived at Benares, he fully utilized his eyes and ears, felt a strong mission which called him to a different scene of action, got an employment as adviser to the Sayyads and again entered the Deccan about the year 1716 in the camp of Sayyad Husain Ali, when the latter was appointed the Subahdar of the Deccan. It was through Shankraji Malhar that Husain Ali made overtures of peace to Shahu. Shankraji came to Satara on deputation, formed, in consultation with Shahu's ministers plans of mutual co-operation and made overtures through his master, the Sayyad, for a defensive alliance between the Marathas and the Emperor, thereby bringing about the eventual grant to Shahu of the three great sanads of Swaraj, Chauthai, and Sardeshmukhi· These grants were first promised to the Peshwa and afterwards confirmed by the Emperor Farrukhsiyar at Delhi in the year 1719. If we thus collect together the various threads of events which were happening in different parts of India, it will facilitate our task of estimating the undercurrents which governed the action of Shahu and his first Peshwa. It will also give us a correct idea of the Maratha Government which the Peshwas created. It can be readily gathered from this explanation that the Maratha constitution as it was worked out, was not of a brand new type, first theoretically conceived and then put into execution, nor was it without plan or premeditation, a mere casual drift or occurrence as has been frequently asserted. No human creation is possible without a preconceived plan. Maratha rule cannot be an altogether accidental creation of a moment's will. They built up their policy on old foundations out of existing materials, which were utilized in the new fabric as much as possible ; and fresh supports and extensions, wherever necessary, convenient and possible, were introduced in course of time, with the result that we are familiar with. Such is usually the case in politics nearly everywhere.

It is said that the Marathas had always their faces to the north. The front gate of the Peshwas' palace faces the north. It is here that they concentrated their ambitions. Bajirao's striking successes against Giridhar Bahadur, Daya Bahadur and Muhammadkhan Bangash in 1729 gave such a shock to the Emperor, his Court and the Rajput princes, that authorized embassies were specially despatched to the Maratha King at Satara in order to ascertain the exact power and intentions of the Maratha leaders.

5. *The brilliant career of Bajirao I.*

Before Balaji Vishvanath was appointed to the Peshwaship in 1713, he had long and keenly watched the Maratha struggle with the Emperor, studied the motives of the principal actors who had won successes, and often kept up secret communication with Shahu during his captivity. It is clear that Shahu did not all at once raise a common individual to his Peshwaship, without fully knowing his family and his antecedents. On the other hand Balaji had already made up his mind that Shahu's presence at the helm of affairs alone could give the desired lead to the nation and save the State from collapse. With remarkable resourcefulness Balaji extricated Shahu out of his enormous difficulties and with his approval and sanction laid down a policy, which was mainly responsible for the rapid expansion of the Maratha Empire. His sons Bajirao and Chimnaji were closely associated with him in the planning of this policy and enthusiastically set themselves to the task of executing it after his rather sudden death in April 1720. It was easier for Balaji to obtain the three sanads from the Emperor, than for his sons to work them in actual practice. The Sayyads were gone, and the astute Nizam-ul-Mulk who had fully imbibed Aurangzeb's hatred for the Marathas, had come on the scene to handle the imperial affairs both in the south and at the Emperor's Court. He strongly opposed the concessions which his master had made under pressure, and engaged the new Peshwa and the other Maratha leaders in an uninterrupted contest in which the Peshwa discovered his chance of distinguishing himself, as he was gifted with a head to plan and a hand to execute.

In order that this struggle may be satisfactorily analysed and set in its proper historical perspective, one must first closely study the chronology of the movements of these two principal actors, Bajirao and Nizam-ul-Mulk, and their helpmates, and grasp the motives with which those movements were undertaken. Dissimulating friendship at one moment, preparing to fight openly at another, always closely watching each other through trusted spies and news-writers, carefully avoiding the sacrifice of money and resources as far as possible, and striking his opponent at a psychological moment, both Bajirao and the Nizam consummately played the game of putting down each other, with the result that the Maratha power was firmly built up, although as we witness to-day, the Nizam's dominion exists and the Maratha one is gone.

Bajirao, exactly 29 years younger than his opponent, started his career with an honest desire to conciliate the Nizam, paid him several personal visits (once in Jan. 1721, again in May 1724 and once more in Dec. 1732). and helped him to establish himself at Aurangabad after putting down Mubarizkhan in the battle of Sakarkhedla in 1724. Thereafter by way of diversion Bajirao made incursions, first into Malwa and then into the Karnatak (1722-1726), trying to feel his way to some decided action, and after a stalemate of two years, both he and the Nizam undertook some arduous and deceptive marches through distant lands, and came to close grips at Palkhed, 20 miles west of Daulatabad, in February 1728, when Bajirao was able to impose the regular payment of the Chauthai and the Sardeshmukhi dues upon his opponent and to make him innocuous at least for some years.

Bajirao at once pushed his success to the utmost advantage. After the Dassara season of 1728 the two brothers prepared for a sudden rush simultaneously into Malwa and Bundelkhand, then governed on behalf of the Emperor by Giridhar Bahadur and Muhammad Khan Bangash respectively. Chimnaji proceeded by the western route through Khandesh and Bajirao through Berar, both collecting contingents on the way and keeping close touch with each other. In the last week of November 1728 Chimnaji reached the Narmada and, having there obtained correct news of the situation and dispositions of Giridhar Bahadur and his cousin Daya Bahadur, he suddenly fell upon the former through an unsuspected pass on 29th November at Amjhera near Mandavgad. Both the imperial nobles fell fighting bravely for their master and yielding an enormous amount of booty to the victor. Three months later Bajirao reached Bundelkhand *via* Gadha Mandala, and, hearing that Muhammad Khan Bangash had attacked Raja Chhatrasal, advanced and routed the former in an action near Jaitpur early in April 1729 and put to flight his cousin Qaim Khan. His brother Chimnaji descended into Gujarat from Malwa, the two together extending Maratha influence right up to the river Jumna. The two brothers proceeded to Satara to receive from their master encomiums for their achievement. These rapid and signal successes at once established the Peshwa's reputation throughout India and gave a clear foretaste to the Emperor, his vassals and allies, of what they were to expect from the Marathas thereafter. The Emperor was so completely overawed that he at once asked Sawai Jaisinh to depute a clever envoy to their Court at Satara. Accordingly Deepsinh, Baghsinh and Mansaram Purohit visited Shahu at Satara, and from thence Nizam-ul-Mulk at Aurangabad in October 1730, and gave an eloquent report of Bajirao's valour and capacity and the strength of king Shahu's position.* Thus the year 1728 marks the starting point of Bajirao's brilliant career. Since then, year after year he obtained successes, now against Janjira, then against Saadat Khan and other imperial grandees, and lastly in 1737 he suddenly fell upon Delhi and disappeared like lightning, striking terror into the capital city of the Mughal Empire. Early next year he once more brought the Nizam to bay at Bhopal, and ended his career while in full youth and vigour, by an abrupt death on the banks of the Narmada in April 1740, leaving the proper completion of his various undertakings to his capable son Balajirao.

6. *The process of Maratha expansion, interchange between north and south.*

I have already detailed the circumstances prevailing at the time of Aurangzeb's death, which brought about a great change in the politics of the Marathas. Although

* Selec. P. D. 10-64.

Shahu had not much chance of success in the beginning, he soon proved a ruler of benevolent instincts in a way suited to the requirements of the time and was able to extend his dominion much beyond the expectation either of himself or of any one else. He succeeded because he followed the policy of non-violence towards Muslims and also because he had no capable rival in his own family. His aunt Tara Bai had a fair amount of sagacity and strength, but being a lady she had necessarily to depend upon subordinates, who often proved faithless. Her son Shivaji was an idiot and her step-son Sambhaji was not much better. Moreover, Shahu gave a free hand, an ample field for action to any and every person that approached him for patronage, which indeed was his most favourite game. Most of the historical families which figure so largely in Maratha history, rose to prominence under the direct encouragement of Shahu, who never entertained any selfish or niggardly motive in his measures and freely promoted all who showed capacity. As Shivaji did not give grants of land for military service, we have hardly any family of his own time now existing and enjoying *Inams*. But under the Saranjami system of the succeeding period, the nature of which I have already fully described, there was plenty of scope for lucrative military service all over the country. The exaction of Chauth supplied the plausible excuse for Maratha bands to undertake distant expeditions. Requests for Maratha help could be easily secured in those days of trouble and insecurity.

For fresh recruits going out from Maharastra, not much education or equipment was needed. Reading, writing and arithmetic of a practical nature, were all that was necessary and could be easily acquired. The cheap Deccani ponies made riding a profession and a pastime for all from the highest to the lowest, not excluding the female sex, for in those days nearly every woman also had to be able to ride and ride well, as a necessary equipment for life and security in case of danger. The memoirs of an English lady named Fanny Park who was invited by Baizabai Sinde (wife of Daulat Rao) in the year 1835, vividly describe the excellent riding and other sports in which Maratha ladies were so highly skilled in those days. Youths of 12 or 14, who in our days hardly finish their school career, flocked to the standard of one or other of the Maratha sardars and soon found plenty of opportunity to prove their merit if they possessed any. A daring deed of courage and heroism was immediately noticed and reported, and received handsome recognition. In fact practical experience in every day affairs with a manly sporting temperament, was all that was needed and proved an immense advantage to all in those days.

In the accounts of the various historical families that I have prepared, one easily notices that the founders are known invariably to have started their roving life at the age of 12 or so, and lived and worked often to a good old age of 70 or more. The open door adventurous life which their profession of arms supplied, conduced both to their health and prosperity. Marathas of all castes, Brahmans including Saraswats and Prabhus (*i.e.*, Kayasthas), all figure prominently in this period of expansion which embraced Shahu's regime. As a rule, the Prabhus with a few exceptions kept to their ancestral profession of writing. The Saraswats were experts in account-keeping and management of household concerns. The Deccani and other Brahmans, whose original occupation before Shivaji's days had been priesthood and scriptural studies, soon adapted themselves to a military profession in which they received easy patronage during the Brahman rule of the able Peshwas. In this connection it is interesting to note the change from priesthood to warfare in the case of the Brahmans, from the manner in which the style of their names changed. The first Peshwa Balaji has been usually known by his familiar name Balajipant Nana; the adjunct *Pant* is a diminutive of *Pandit*, expressing that the person at start was a mere scholar versed in Sanskrit studies; but the second Peshwa began to be called Baji *Rao* and not Baji *Pant*, expressing a Kshatriya or military profession. The third Peshwa, also named Balaji, has been called Balaji *Rao* and not Balaji *Pant*. This significant change in title has affected nearly all the Brahmans, and implies a change of profession brought about by the Peshwas.

Shahu's regime supplied real *Swarajya* to all kinds of people. In the wake of military conquest, Maratha life expanded in various directions. Writers, bankers, accountants, artisans, builders, painters, priests, bards, servants of all kinds, came into requisition, and Maratha settlements quickly rose in all important towns in the north. One has only to cast a passing look at towns like Baroda, Nagpur, Indore, Dhar, Dewas, Ujjain, Jhansi and others, in order to be convinced how these became essentially Maratha colonies deliberately transplanted in the midst of Hindi surroundings of old. Maratha life in the Deccan itself received a fresh enrichment and influence by contact with the north. Many articles of use and luxury, clothes, ornaments, household furniture, military accoutrements, paintings, articles of dietary, music, dancing, court etiquette, the pomp and manners of the northern nobility, were quickly introduced and greedily imitated all over the Deccan, as the papers of the time amply show. The Marathi language itself has received material addition in vocabulary and expression. Numerous letters have been published containing demands made by residents of the Deccan for various kinds of articles and supplies, not excluding even dancing girls from the north, who came to be in much requisition at the Courts of the Pehswa and his sardars. In my opinion, this interchange between the north and the south has been altogether healthy and beneficial, and tended to enrich the life of both, although it must be said that the frequent Maratha exactions of tributes and taxes must have drained the north of its wealth to some extent at the initial stages of the Maratha conquest ; but even here, it must be remembered, that the money remained in the country, did not go out of it and ultimately benefited the people in one way or another. The Peshwas were never spendthrifts, and did not waste money over useless shows or costly living. Later on, when the Maratha leaders established more or less permanent capitals in the north and the west, the Maratha exactions lost their former unpleasant character and assumed the aspect of the usual taxes, which all people have to pay to their Government everywhere. One insistent demand, be it noted, from the Deccan on the north, was for manuscripts of old Sanskrit works of various kinds, of poetry, literature, scriptures, *puranas*, etc. Revenue accounts, land measurements and various governmental functions of a purely Deccani type, were freely introduced into the north. Religious functions in particular came to be modelled on the Maharastrian pattern. This interchange between the north and the south and its effects on the social and economic life of the people as a whole, deserve a special study.

7. *Shahu's personality and character.*

King Shahu's memory is still held in high reverence in Maharastra. He could truly boast of being one who never did a wrong to anybody. Thousands of people had cause to remember him as their benefactor and blessed him in all sincerity. Although there was not much love lost between him and his cousin Sambhaji of Kolhapur. Shahu never allowed his Peshwa or any other official to molest Sambhaji for any fault or dereliction of his. It is said that Sambhaji once hired assassins and employed them to murder Shahu, but when they came into his presence, they dropped their arms at the very sight of him and did not dare to raise their hands against him. Upon learning their intention, Shahu rewarded them and sent them back to Sambhaji with a message, that they were brave men and should be employed on a better mission. The founders of the houses of Nagpur, of Akalkot, of Dhar, Indore, Ujjain, Baroda and other places, were all young boys whose capacity and valour were first recognized and rewarded by Shahu. Vithal Shivdev of Vinchur and Naro Shankar of Malegaum, who later figured in history were brought into prominence at the instance of Shahu. The ancestor of the great family of the Hingnes, who were long the Peshwas' agents at the Court of Delhi and who carried on banking business in addition, was one Mahadev Bhat, the family priest of the Peshwas at Nasik, who travelled to Delhi in the company of the first Peshwa and was posted there by him to look after the Maratha interests, a task which he long carried out with phenomenal success. This change from pure priesthood to conspicuous diplomacy is particularly significant and may be taken as an instance of how with increasing facilities for occupation, a nation's life in general becomes enriched and expanded all round.* If I have to compare Shahu with any modern ruler whom we know, I would liken him to Queen Victoria, who could detect the best merit in her ministers and requisition it for the service of the nation, who could be at once strong, simple and benevolent, who could tactfully check, when occasion required, the rebellious spirit in her servants and whose memory has been hallowed by the unbroken success and prosperity which attended her rule.

Shahu treated all people alike, had a soft corner in his heart for everyone who approached him and had no tinge of caste prejudice in his nature or policy. Any merit or capacity was at once recognized. Although he did not personally lead distant expeditions, he kept a close and strict watch over the actions of his subordinates to whom he had allotted separate spheres of influence. He called them to account for any wrong or misdeed that they committed, reprimanded them, punished them, rewarded them, composed their mutual quarrels and adjusted their disputes by calling them to his presence at Satara for personal explanation, reconciliation, or settlement. One typical instance will suffice. In 1731 Shahu's Senapati Trimbakrao Dabhade joined the Nizam with a view to putting down the ambitious Peshwa Baji Rao, of whose growing influence and personal valour the Senapati had grown extremely jealous. He openly flouted Shahu's orders to support Baji Rao in his forward policy ; and when it became necessary to call him to account for openly joining the enemy's cause, Shahu asked Baji Rao to lead an expedition against him, and bring him a captive to his presence at Satara. Now, this Dabhade was also of an equally spirited tem-

* Incidentally one comes to realize in this connection why Britain tries every nerve to keep India in her possession.

perament and would not give up the game lightly. An open fight took place between these two highest officials of Shahu,—his Prime Minister and his Commander-in-Chief,—near Dabhoi (Baroda) in the month of April 1731, in which, at an evil moment as the two armies came almost to a death grip, a random shot now known to have been fired by a traitor's hand in the Senapati's own camp, killed him instantaneously, giving on that account a complete victory to the Peshwa.

The moral effect of this incident was indeed serious and convulsed the whole nation ; it was a grievous sight that these two brave men, serving the same master and equally bound to guard his interests, engaged in a deadly fight in which the Senapati was killed. His mother, Umabai, a proud and spirited lady for whom Shahu entertained great personal reverence, at once visited him at Satara and demanded vengeance upon the Peshwa. Shahu immediately called Bajirao to his presence and composed the feud in his own peculiar way. The Senapati had his hereditary seat at Talegaum near Poona, where the whole party including Shahu and his Court repaired. A throne was constructed out of a heap of silver rupees and was occupied by Shahu, who called Umabai and Baji Rao to his presence, gave a sword to the lady and asked her to cut off Baji Rao's head as he knelt before her, with her own hand in retaliation for her son's death. The sight was impressive and pathetic. Baji Rao was pardoned by the lady. The two feasted each other and exchanged cordial greetings. Terms of settlement were drawn up. Umabai's second son Yashvant Rao was made Senapati and the incident closed. Unfortunately, Yashvant Rao was given to drink and proved utterly incapable of holding his position, so that thenceforth the Senapati became a non-entity and the Peshwa scored in the game for all practical purposes. A similar dispute had for years developed between Raghuji Bhosle and Peshwa Balaji Bajirao, which was similarly composed later in 1743.

Incidents like these are not rare in Shahu's time and show the peculiarly parental manner in which he behaved to his people, an example to all of plain living and honest dealing. But his ignorance of the political issues before the nation, inevitably led to the concentration of all power of initiative and action in the hands of his capable Peshwa ; in fact, Shahu had a kind of superstitious faith in the success of whatever the members of this Peshwa family undertook, and whole-heartedly supported them, so that the concerns of an expanding empire might not sit heavily on himself. The Peshwas on their part served him with equal devotion and loyalty.

Shahu's first Peshwa Balaji Vishvanath died unexpectedly in 1720, leaving the completion of his half finished work to his son Baji Rao, then only 19 years of age, whose capacity had not been tried before or recognized in any quarter ; but Shahu, acting on intuition rather than reason, conferred the Peshwaship on him in preference to older and tried veterans, who claimed the post. Shahu put them all aside and made a choice which was more than justified by later events. There is always a difference of opinion as to the wisdom of making public offices hereditary in a family, and I am not prepared to justify the practice. One caution should, however, be borne in mind in this connection, *viz.*, that we must not judge matters of those days by our present day standards. Baji Rao died an early death in 1740 after 20 years' arduous service. His son, named Balaji, commonly called Nana Saheb, was only 18 when he was appointed to the Peshwaship ; with the declining age and impaired health of Shahu, the master and the servant showed a marked contrast both in age and capacity, in the management of the growing concerns of an expanding Maratha rule, that was fast attaining first-rate importance among all the powers of India including the Emperor. All the four early Peshwas carried on a continuous policy which had been laid down in the beginning, and risked all they had in accomplishing the great object of building up a Hindu empire, which Shivaji first formulated for adoption by the nation,—so that the 60 years' period from 1713 to 1773 forms one unbroken chain of events, measures and schemes all calculated to secure that one single aim, and can be said to be the brightest period of Maratha power, in which the nation and its leaders put forth the very best ability they possessed, and in which peace, prosperity, and orderly government were attained by the peoples of India, as has been verified and asserted even by the critical western writers.*

This period exemplifies merely the working out of the three sanads obtained from the Emperor by the first Peshwa in 1719 and was not interrupted, so far as the main current of political events goes, by the death of Shahu which occurred in December 1749. Although the policy of the Maratha Raj was not affected by this event, some critics, ignorant of the situation which can now be studied correctly from the original papers, have detected in it sinister motives on the part of the third Peshwa, whom they charge with deliberately usurping the power of the Chhatrapatis. I for one believe that the Peshwa boldly relieved the embarrassment created by Shahu's death and saved the situation at a critical moment in the fortunes of the nation. The situation at the death of Shahu, involved risks more or less similar to those of the Mughal Court at the time of Aurangzeb's death ; but it is creditable to the third Peshwa that he did not allow it to affect or interrupt the forward policy which had been already adopted. This point requires a closer examination.

8. *Shahu's last days, the question of succession and how the Peshwa handled the situation*

In the year 1743 when the Peshwa Balaji Bajirao was engaged in the north in wresting Malwa from the Emperor and bringing Bengal under his influence, a sudden illness of Shahu called him back abruptly to the Deccan, to handle a situation complicated by the usual palace intrigues of a Court, where no constitution save the will of a powerful king had reigned supreme for over a generation. Shahu had two queens but no issue from either ; the future was dark ; the usual infirmities caused by age and worry had unnerved his otherwise robust

* See Sir Richard Temple's Oriental Experience p. 402.

constitution. For five long years he lay dying, a period which the Peshwa had to waste at the headquarters and which he could have profitably utilized in completing his task in northern India, so as possibly to avert the future complications in the north, created by the appearance of Ahmad Shah Abdali on the scene. At the age of 25, this young Peshwa was called upon to deal with a severe crisis, involving the fate of the Maratha State, and, for a time endangering its very existence. The two queens of Shahu and his aunt Tarabai, who was a prisoner in the fort of Satara, started intrigues about the succession and the future government of the State, when they felt that Shahu was going to pass away. Shahu had about him then more than a dozen competent and experienced advisers, sardars and generals, whom he freely and repeatedly consulted and with whom he long discussed the subject of selection of an heir to succeed him.

The Peshwa's own plan was to bring Sambhaji from Kolhapur and entrust the Satara Raj to him, thus bringing about a desirable union, like that of England and Scotland in 1707, and removing at least one cause of constant friction in Maratha politics. But Shahu was entirely opposed to having for his successor a cousin whom he had hated all his life. When other competent youths were being looked for in the collateral Bhosle family for adoption, Tarabai suggested the name of a grandson of hers named Ram Raja, born of her imbecile son Shivaji who had died in 1726. She alleged that she had concealed this Ram Raja since his childhood, for fear of an attempt on his life by his uncle Sambhaji, in an out of the way village, far away from home, and impressed upon Shahu the wisdom of selecting this nearest heir for his successor, as he was born in a direct line from the great Shivaji. In the unsafe circumstances of the plots and complications then prevailing at Satara, it was not thought advisable to bring Ram Raja there at once from his concealed refuge ; and Shahu after due consideration wrote two small notes, now termed his will, in his own hand, providing for Ram Raja being raised to the throne after his death, and enjoining the Peshwa to conduct the affairs of the State as before.The two notes have been printed in facsimile and are admitted to be in Shahu's own hand, so that they can conclusively prove that the Peshwa played no personal game in selecting the heir according to the terms of the will as is often alleged on insufficient evidence. In fact, it now appears, that the contents of these wills and the commands laid down in them by Shahu, were in no way conducive to any selfish object on the part of the Peshwa ; he carried out his duty to the best of his power and a spirit of filial obligation. The pre-eminence of the Peshwas both in arms and diplomacy has been universally acknowledged and, as they actually asserted more than once, they could easily have carved out for themselves an independent field of work like the other Maratha chiefs and remained aloof, as did Raghuji Bhosle of Nagpur, from interfering with the affairs of the central Government, a task in which they stood to gain little, but to court blame and displeasure from the various parties after Shahu's demise.

With all the liberality and softness of his heart, Shahu never realized that a State and its Government, like other human affairs, are progressive, that they must change as times and circumtances change. He laid down an impossible condition, "Do not give up an old practice do not start a new one." This particularly referred to the Saranjams or jagirs which the various sardars were enjoying. When the Peshwa came to manage the affairs of the State after Shahu's death, he found that most of the jagirdars would not supply efficient troops for State service, but would squander away their incomes on matters of personal enjoyment. If the Peshwa took severe steps against them, they showed a rebellious spirit and would not serve him faithfully. Unfortunately Ram Raja, who became Chhatrapati in pursuance of Shahu's last wishes, proved incapable and was later on openly declared by Tarabai herself to be an impostor and not her grandson at all. She had played this game in order to secure power into her own hands, a result which the Peshwa was shrewd enough to prevent. They severely disagreed and after wasting three precious years in useless wrangling, the Peshwa kept both Tarabai and Ram Raja in check at Satara and renewed his projected work of conquest in spite of them. Of course, this involved a waste of two years' precious time and energy in guarding against a domestic trouble, which would have burst out any time on the part of many rebellious spirits. It has also been urged against the Peshwa that he purposely brought to the throne an incompetent Chhatrapati ; but as we have shown, it was all the working of Tarabai alone and the Peshwa had no hand in it, although like a shrewd politician he did not afterwards hesitate to utilize the situation to his best advantage. Looking at the matter impartially at this distance of time, one can easily realize that, if the Peshwa had an able Chhatrapati at least of the type of Rajaram or Shahu to order and guide him from above, as well as to share his troubles and responsibilities, he would have been able to achieve far greater advances in his foreign policy than he was actually able to do.

9. *Change in Maratha Government, the Peshwa's mistake*

There is, however, no doubt that the death of Shahu brought about a great change in the Maratha adminstration. Satara lost its regal importance and Poona became the seat of the Maratha Government. Henceforth the Chhatrapati became a nonentity. Ram Raja was discovered to be illegitimate after he had occupied the throne for several years, during which time, marriage alliances and social amenities with him had freely taken place which could not be revoked.* When he died in 1777, the Maratha State was fast declining, being involved in a deadly war with the British power, and no one had time or leisure to restore the Chhatrapati to power and influence. But of this I shall have occasion to speak later. It is enough for our

* See Burhanji Mohite's complaint in P. D. S. VI.

immediate purpose to remember that the Peshwa inherited only a heavy responsibility from Shahu, but none of the royal influence and prestige, which were more or less personal and inseparable from the position of the Chhatrapati as the head of the State and occupant of Shivaji's throne. For instance, the eight hereditary ministers of Shivaji and some of the older sardars enjoyed their former positions even at this time and held jagirs but did not readily submit to the orders of the Peshwa, whom they looked upon as their equal, if not subordinate, while unity of command and strict discipline are always most essential for the execution of any State affair. In this respect the Peshwa and his successors always found it most difficult to exact obedience to their orders : while the Raja of Kolhapur and some older jagirdars ever proved a thorn in their side, whenever foreign dangers assumed a threatening aspect. The normal Maratha character has had all along a rebellious spirit in it : its greatest weakness perhaps is an impatience of control and defiance of authority. Shivaji himself had often quietly to put up with this insubordinate spirit, as when he found that there were some old Maratha sardars who would not render obedience to the Bhosles or occupy a seat lower than the throne, which Shivaji had raised for himself. In fact, half the energy of the Maratha rulers had ever been spent in checking and punishing this centrifugal tendency, which was also, as we know, responsible to a great extent for bringing about their downfall.

When Shahu was crowned at Satara he could not control his rebel Senapati Chandrasen Jadhav or Rao Rambha Nimbalkar and they both joined the standard of the Nizam under whom they still hold jagirs of their own. The story of the revolt of Shahu's next Senapati Dabhade has been already dealt with. Raghuji Bhosle and Peshwa Balajirao fought open battles in Central India and Bengal. Immediately on the death of Shahu the Peshwa had to face a strong rebellion of the combined armies of Yashavantrao Dabhade and Damaji Gaikwad. Malharrao Holkar was reported to have been instrumental in bringing about the great disaster of Panipat by openly supporting the intriguing Najib Khan Rohilla. Peshwa Madhav Rao I had to waste three precious years of his life in putting down first the defection of his own uncle Raghunath Rao and then a combination of the Bhosle of Nagpur, the Pratinidhi and Gopalrao Patwardhan. Raghunath Rao's fight for the Peshwaship and his open acceptance of British help led to the great First Maratha War, which nearly destroyed the independence of the Maratha State. And lastly, it is well known how Lord Wellesley and his brother the famous Duke dexterously divided the Maratha potentates one against the others and subjugated each separately. This duty of the central authority in bringing to book rebellious elements is unpleasant at all times and everywhere, but it became doubly so when for practical purposes the Peshwa took the Chhatrapati's position as the head of the Maratha Government without possessing the royal prestige. This point became still more delicate when, upon the murder of Peshwa Narayan Rao, all power devolved upon Nana Phadnis who, however shrewd and wise in statecraft, was in official parlance a mere Phadnis or head-accountant of the Peshwa's office. This was the inner motive of Mahadji Sindia and others in often refusing obedience to Nana, a difference which threatened serious consequences and which the good sense of the two alone ultimately managed to close. This dwindling of Government's power and prestige at each crisis in the Maratha fortunes, deserves to be carefully noted, as it was largely responsible, apart from other and extraneous causes, for the fact that the Maratha Power ultimately succumbed to the British so easily. Just as the Peshwas, at the death of Shahu came into possession of the regal power because they were capable, so did Nana Phadnis come to wield full power when the Peshwas' family had no capable member to represent it. Although in human affairs it is capacity that ultimately rules, forms and ceremonials have also their own influence in politics. Hence each succeeding delegation came to lose much of the force of the original. What a student of history has to note is that one must carefully consider all the factors in the situation before blaming the Peshwas or others for usurpation of the Chhatrapati's power.

But the policy of the third Peshwa Balajirao was found wanting when he came face to face with the British power. In fact, in comparing the Maratha politicians with the British, we must rank the former far lower in the scale. The period 1750-61 is doubtless most eventful and revolutionary for the fortunes of India, for in this period the British, in the famous Seven Years' War, finally put down their rivals the French, conquered two large provinces, Bengal and Madras, and nearly completed erecting the net of their supremacy round the east coast and as far up as Allahabad in the north. At this time the Peshwa made two serious mistakes. He took British help to crush the Maratha navy headed by the Angria, his own naval commander, and secondly, he utterly neglected to support the Bhosle's claims in Bengal, when Siraj-ud-Daula was being hard pressed by the British, before the battle of Plassey. Bengal had long ago been conquered by Raghuji and subjected to an annual payment of the Chauth in return for which the Marathas were bound to help its Subahdar. When the British turned their arms against Siraj-ud-Daula, it was the duty of the Peshwa to send immediate help to him. In 1756 the Peshwa's hands were practically free ; his position was secure, and he was at the time the most powerful potentate in India. A move on his part then against the British both in the Karnatak and in Bengal, would have at once checked their advance.

But the Peshwa paid undue attention to the politics of Delhi and contracted unnecessary enmity with the Abdali, bringing upon himself the disaster of Panipat. He had no business to go beyond the Sutlaj into the Punjab for conquest so recklessly. But Panipat decided the future course of the history of India. The Marathas and the Muhammadans weakened each other in that deadly conflict, facilitating the aims of the British for Indian supremacy. It seems to have been quite within the power of the Peshwa to have successfully interfered in the contest both of Plassey and the Karnatak, and thus prevented British supremacy. But he did not go personally into the north, entrusted important developments of policy to incompetent subordinates, and hardly understood the real nature of the British game, so that he was found wanting in sagacity and length of vision at a crucial moment. If he had understood all-India politics, he would have acted otherwise. This point is clearly established by the results of the Seven Years' War between the French and the British, and the easy manner in which all the Muhammadan potentates, the Emperor, Mir Jafar, Mir Qasim and Vazir Shuja-ud-Daula of Oudh were quickly disposed of by the British, who became masters of the entire field for all practical purposes.

LECTURE V

DEVELOPMENT OF MUSLIM-MARATHA CONTEST

1, *The battle of Panipat,—antecedent causes*

The antecedents of this great event go back to a decade or two, and it can be clearly set out in a chain of causation. The disaster of Panipat appears now to be the legitimate consequence of Maratha commitments deliberately undertaken by the first three Peshwas, all of whom vigorously tried to complete the ideal of Hindu-pad Padshahi, first concieved but left unfinished by the great founder. This ambition of the Peshwas brought them into increasing conflict with the various chiefs and potentates, each of whom, like the Nizam, losing the support of the central authority of the Emperor, tried to carve out an independent principality for himself and seize a slice of the falling Empire. The deadly blow dealt to that empire by Nadir Shah in 1739, made the position of the Emperor so precarious that he lay at the mercy of any invader of superior strength ; and when he found that the Peshwas had proved themselves capable of dictating terms to the various warring elements in India, he decided to seek their protection in order to maintain his position. The Peshwas had already in 1743 practically wrested the Subahs of Malwa and Bundelkhand from the Emperor's hands and imposed their contributions upon the bordering Rajput States, the principal among whom then was Jaypur which was ruled by Sawai Jaysinh. His death in the same year started the usual war of succession between the rival claimants, which the shrewd Peshwa was not slow to turn to his own advantage. He at once deputed his two ablest generals, Ranoji Sindia and Malharrao Holkar, the founders of the two present Maratha States in Malwa, to adjust the dispute about the vacant throne of Jaipur, if necessary by force of arms. The Peshwa could not long be present in the north to guide the course of events owing to the troubles created at Satara by Shahu's old age and declining health, and the movements of Nizam ul-Mulk who was at that time trying to strengthen his hold on the Karnatak.

The deaths of important personages have been politically convulsive at all times and places, and in this respect the middle of the eighteenth century proved to be a period of peculiar unrest for India, and materially changed the course of its history. The student will therefore do well to note carefully the following events :—

21-9-1743	Sawai Jaysinh dies.
9-6-1747	Nadir Shah is murdered and Ahmad Shah Abdali rises to power.
15-4-1748	Emperor Muhammad Shah dies.
21-5-1748	Nizam-ul-Mulk dies.
21-6-1749	Abhay Sinh of Jodhpur dies.
14-12-1749	King Shahu dies.
5-12-1750	Nasirjang is murdered.
12-12-1750	Ishwarisinh of Jaipur commits suicide.

These events created a confused situation which we must carefully analyse, particularly as regards the events occurring at the Courts of Delhi and Satara. Jaisinh's death started a war of succession which lasted practically from 1745 to 1750. Similarly, the Emperor's death in 1748 involved Vazir Safdar Jang in a war with the Rohillas which continued from November 1748 to April 1752. Sindia and Holkar whom the Peshwa had stationed in the north with full instructions to handle the situation and with ample freedom to act as occasion and emergency required, weakened the Maratha cause by their personal jealousies, and between them managed to destroy all the friendship and good feeling which the first two Peshwas under inspiration from Shahu had sedulously cultivated with the Rajput princes. This alienation of Rajput sympathies by Sindia and Holkar must be borne in mind as one of the predisposing factors which ultimately frustrated the Maratha attempts to estabilsh a Hindu Empire for

India. The Jaipur ruler Ishwarisinh was so exasperated at the Maratha encroachments on his dominions, that he found life intolerable and, along with three of his wives, put an end to his life by a cobra-bite, at which twenty of his maid-servants followed the same course on the Raja's funeral pyre. This occurrence was so keenly resented by the Rajputs all round, that they inflicted frightful atrocities upon the Maratha troops at the time visiting Jaipur to exact the Maratha demands. The whole affair is eloquently described in a letter* dated 21-2-1751, which shows how the Rajputs and the Marathas became bitter enemies thereafter. Had Shahu been at the head of affairs, he would not have allowed such wanton aggression.

Apart from the injudicious Maratha dealings with the Rajputs, the Peshwa undertook the more difficult task of helping the Emperor out of his embarrassments, which the invasions of Ahmad Shah Abdali had created. After Nadir Shah's death, his successor Ahmad Shah laid claim to the Punjab as part of his inheritance, entered India, seized Lahore in January 1748 ; but as he advanced to Sirhind, he was routed by Prince Ahmad at Manupur on 11th March 1748 and compelled to retreat ; but the Emperor's death occurring shortly after, resulted in concentrating all power in the hands of Vazir Mansur Ali Khan Safdar Jang, who used this opportunity for crushing the Rohillas as they were his troublesome neighbours. Thus an open war ensued between them which lasted for over two years. In this war the Vazir, being unable to cope with the strength of the Rohillas, invited the help of Sindia and Holkar who were then at Jaipur, and with the united forces inflicted a crushing defeat upon his opponents at the battle of Husainpur on 19-4-1751, thereby establishing Maratha prestige in the politics of Delhi. As a counterpoise, the worsted Rohillas looked to the Abdali king as their saviour and induced him to invade India and put down the power of the Vazir. He

* No. 31 of Selection P. D. 2.

was only too eager to wipe out his defeat of four years ago at Sirhind, entered India early in 1752, and this time annexed the two frontier provinces of Lahore and Multan. This loss of the Punjab was bitterly felt by the Emperor, who with the advice of the new Vazir Ghazi-uddin Imad-ul-Mulk openly accepted Maratha protection, contracted an agreement with Sindia and Holkar on 12 April 1752 and granted them the *Chauth* over all the northern territories of the Empire in return for their promise of service. This proceeding gave rise to a perpetual hostility between the king of the Afghans and the Peshwa, each in turn trying to establish control over the Emperor and his capital. The natural result was a long drawn contest between them, which was ultimately decided at Panipat.

2. *Abdali accepts the challenge*

Sindia and Holkar, it may be realized, evidently committed the Peshwa rather rashly to an undertaking which proved too much for their scanty resources, particularly when the Peshwa had on his hand other momentous issues in the south. The defence of the vast territories of northern India stretching from Attock to the environs of Bengal, against both internal revolt and foreign aggression was no easy task. The Peshwa's undertaking was indeed the fore-runner of the famous Subsidiary System of Lord Wellesley and would have proved fairly successful, had the two agents of the Peshwa, Sindia and Holkar, acted in complete accord with each other. Their mutual jealousy and antagonism ruined the project. The Peshwa was too much occupied in consolidating his position in the south either to pay a personal visit himself to the north, or to despatch a competent person with sufficient funds and forces for carrying out the pledges given to the Emperor. The Maratha undertaking was an open challenge to the Afghan king, who was urged thereon by Najib-ud-Daula, an astute Rohilla chief, who represented the anti-Maratha faction at the Court of Delhi. Thus came into being a contest which had to be legitimately fought out on the principle of a trial of strength. Having contracted the agreement for the defence of the Emperor, Sindia and Holkar immediately returned to the south, explained matters to the Peshwa and brought a strong force to Delhi, headed by the Peshwa's brother Raghoba. During 1754 the combined Maratha armies vanquished all opposition to their plans and, on the advice of Ghaziuddin, having deposed the incompetent Emperor, installed Alamgir II. on the throne and returned to the south after effecting a settlement of the outstanding problems. The Abdali Shah was not slow to act. He soon learned from Najib-ud-Daula all that the Marathas had accomplished, and having formed his plans, descended upon Delhi in the early months of 1757, carried all opposition before him and in revenge this time went a step further. From Delhi he proceeded southward sacked the Hindu shrines and the town of Mathura, and devastated the country right upto Agra. He however found the heat intolerable and leaving Delhi on 2nd April went back to his country after committing frightful atrocities on the way.

3. *Dattaji Sindia killed*

This bold proceeding on the part of Abdali roused the Peshwa to a sense of the situation. He had already achieved unprecedented success in the Karnatak and did not think it a serious business to enter into a contest with the Afghan enemy in the north. Even while Abdali was entering India, the Peshwa again despatched his brother Raghoba with a large force from the Deccan. The latter entered Delhi in August and next year marched into the Punjab, clearing the intervening territory of all vestiges of the Afghan conquest. Before Raghoba had time to consolidate the Maratha position in the Punjab and establish strong outposts against any future cotingency, he was called away to the south by the Peshwa, leaving the situation to subordinate and self-seeking individuals. This was Najib-ud-Daula's opportunity. Fully inspired by hatred for the increasing Maratha penetration, he collected all the Rohilla resources for a heroic struggle, entreated Abdali for an early return, and strongly prepared to oppose the Maratha armies, should they happen to enter Delhi again. The Peshwa was too much engrossed with the affairs in the south to pay personal attention to the development of events at the imperial Court. Holkar was in Rajputana and Dattaji Sindia, a rather rash and reckless soldier who was alone handling the situation at Delhi, was unable to deal a timely blow to the growing intrigues and activities of Najib. At the end of 1759 the Abdali Shah made a sudden sweep into the Punjab, and having quickly effected a strong combination with the Rohilla chiefs, attacked Dattaji by crossing to the right side of the Jumna and killed him outright on January 10, 1760. This year, however, the Shah did not undertake his usual summer return to his own country, but remained in India for the whole year, completing his measures not only for the defence of the Mughal throne, but for inflicting a crushing blow upon the Marathas, if they dared to come and face him once more.

4. *Sadashivrao Bhau beaten*

And this is exactly what happened. The news of the sad event of Dattaji Sindia's defeat and death at the hands of Abdali was not long in reaching the Peshwa. He received it with gloomy forebodings in the midst of the flush of the victory he had obtained over the Nizam at Udgir. He quickly prepared to meet the challenge. He collected a large army near Ahmadnagar, brought together most of his veteran commanders and leaders of contingents, organized a strong park of artillery under the famous expert Ibrahim Khan Gardi trained by Bussy, and quickly despatched them under the leadership of his own cousin Sadashivrao Bhau with instructions to finally dispose of the troublesome Afghan combination. This grand expedition left the banks of the Godavari on the 14th March 1760 and exactly ten months to the day, on the 14th January, 1761, met its final doom at Panipat. Having crossed the Chambal at the end of May, the impetuous Bhau reached the banks of the river Gambhira to the south of Agra, ardently desiring to cross the Jumna and get into grips with Abdali who had cantoned his forces at Anupshahar, not far from the present Aligarh. But early rains had flooded the stream so heavily that it caused the Bhau and his army a detention of a full month on its bank. Finding the Jumna utterly impassable, the Maratha armies advanced upon Delhi, of which they took an easy possession on 1st August 1760, and which the Abdali on the opposite bank was extremely mortified at his inability to succour. Two months passed and yet there was no prospect for either combatant to cross the floods in order to encounter each other. The gigantic armies ate up the whole territory for their food, and when further stay was found impossible, the Bhau proceeded along the river to the north as far as Kunjpura, an outpost on the homeward route of Abdali, which, although strongly garrisoned, surrendered into Maratha hands without much effort. Here the Bhau performed the national festivity of the Dussera on 19th October with a triumph and splendour hardly equalled ever before or since. He then prepared to cross the Jumna higher up, but was surprised to learn that the Abdali had forded the river to the right side with all his troops, baggage and artillery at Bagpat, about 20 miles north of Delhi, between 26 and 28 October, thus intercepting the Maratha communications with Delhi and further south. The operations involved for Abdali also a break of communication with his Afghan home. It will thus be realized that the strategy of Panipat depended mainly on the skill and practice of successfully crossing large rivers, a type of warfare in which Dattaji Sindia was twice baffled the year before, but in which the Abdali Shah with his repeated experience not only of all the rivers of the Punjab, but of those of Afghanistan and Central Asia, was more than a match for the Bhau, who never had experience of such large scale operations in the south.

The Bhau quickly retraced his steps from Kunjpura and hurried towards the south to meet the Afghans; but realizing that his path was effectually blocked, he pitched his camp with the town of Panipat at his back ; while the Afghans formed themselves in battle array at Sonpat about 20 miles further south. Each of the two combatants had a fighting strength reaching nearly half a lac of souls, with double or treble that number of non-combatants on the Maratha side. The opposing armies lay facing each other for full two months and a half. At the beginning of this period, the Marathas were certainly superior in spirit and provisions, and it is yet an unsolved mystery why the Bhau did not at once attack Abdali, who was at first considerably weaker. An eye-witness pithily reported on 5th November that the " Abdali Shah could not reach home as his way is blocked by the Marathas, could not stay where he is for want of food, and could not fight them with any hope of success." But in generalship Abdali was doubtless an unequalled tactician of his day and could easily checkmate the Bhau. He gradually succeeded in cutting off the supply of provisions that reached the Maratha camp and compelling his opponents to offer battle on his own terms out of sheer desperation. The Bhau failed to establish contact with the Sikhs who were bitter enemies of the Afghan invader and would gladly have offered succour to the Marathas.* The Bhau's situation became so critical towards the beginning of January that on the 14th of the month, he was compelled to bring out his large army for a final attack. When the two met, a terrible battle ensued from nine o'clock in the morning for more than six hours, at the end of which a random shot killed the Peshwa's son on his elephant and turned the scales against the Marathas. Moved by the piteous sight of his dead nephew the Bhau lost self-control, rushed recklessly into the thick of the fight and was heard of no more. The victorious Afghans, chafing under the terrible losses which they had suffered during the day, showed no mercy to their vanquished foes. Thousands were cut to pieces, particularly the helpless non-combatants, and only a few escaped with life under cover of the thickening darkness following the short winter day. The flower of the Mara-

---

*See Sardesai Com. Vol. P. 280.

tha army with most of their veteran commanders perished either on the battlefield or of their wounds or at the hands of the peasantry. Large numbers of non-combatants were fearfully massacred. The news of the disaster reached the Peshwa in Malwa a week later and so unsettled his mind that he pined away to death within a few months. The Rajputs could have certainly eased the desperate situation of the Maratha forces; but they deliberately chose to remain passive onlookers.

5. *Results of the battle*

The battle of Panipat is usually understood by most writers to have given a final blow to the rising power of the Marathas. This I think is far from being the case. The loss was doubtless heavy so far as man-power was concerned; but beyond this, the disaster did not materially affect the Maratha fortunes. A younger generation arose to replace quickly the losses suffered at Panipat and so far as the Afghans were concerned, they did not gain anything by their victory. Ahmad Shah, already worn out by a long and harassing campaign of 18 months and not caring any longer to trust Najib-ud-Daula or his lukewarm allies, early in March 1761 took his leave of the Indian plains which had brought him no material profit. The Marathas made good their fortunes ten years later, when the next Peshwa and his spirited generals including Mahadji Sindia brought the legitimate Emperor back to Delhi and installed him on his hereditary throne under Maratha protection, thus fulfilling to the letter the written undertaking of 1752, and indirectly also the grand ideal of Hindu-pad-Padshahi for which the Peshwas had been striving from the beginning of their regime. The declining point of Maratha fortunes began not on the day that brought upon the Marathas the disaster of Panipat, but the day on which their best and most highly qualified ruler, Peshwa Madhavrao I. died a premature death in 1772. The great historian of the Marathas corroborates this view explicitly when he writes that "the plains of Panipat were not more fatal to the Maratha Empire than the early end of this excellent prince." Writes Major

Evans Bell : " Even the battle of Panipat was a triumph and a glory for the Marathas. They fought in the cause of India for the Indians, while the great Muhammadan princes of Delhi, of Oudh and the Deccan stood aside intriguing and trimming : and though the Marathas were defeated, the victorious Afghans retired and never again interfered with the affairs of India."

But in a different sense the battle of Panipat did verily prove a turning point in Indian history. In the middle of the 18th century, there were two strong parties contending for the mastery of India, the rising Marathas and the waning Muslims. A third power, the British, was just rising on the Indian horizon. The first two so weakened each other by their mutual struggles culminating in Panipat that the field was left clear for the third. The learned author of the *Origin of Bombay* (Dr. Gerson da Cunha) has fully grasped this point when he says that " the fall of the Angrias and the disaster of Panipat freed the British from the thraldom of insidious neighbours and hastened their rise." This is amply corroborated by the easy manner in which four years after Panipat, Clive obtained the Diwani of Bengal, *i.e.*, practically the mastery of that rich province and consequently of India. Orissa had then been subjugated by the Bhosles of Nagpur, and had the Peshwas been victorious at Panipat, one feels certain that neither the Nagpur Bhosles nor the Peshawa would have allowed Bengal to slip out of their hands so easily, leaving Clive the unquestioned master of north-eastern India.

6. *A Muslim view of Maratha conquests*

While I have tried to explain as clearly as I could the aims and objects of Maratha policy from Shivaji down to the Peshwas, I must in justice to history not omit to record what the Muslims felt all along. The passage quoted below will supply their view.

Raghunath Yadav, a clerk on the Peshwas' establishment and author of a Marathi Chronicle describing the affair of Panipat within two years of that event, puts into the mouth of Abdali the following remonstrance which he had forwarded with his envoys to Bhausahib, the Commander-in-Chief of the Maratha armies. On p. 19 of the Chronicle is summarized what may be taken as a substantially correct statement of the Maratha ideal of the Hindu-pad-Padshahi. How a religious twist was deliberately lent to a purely political struggle, is clearly visible throughout. Says Abdali :—

"You Marathas have grown intolerably aggressive and have wantonly overrun the imperial territories of Rajputana, the Punjab up to Kashmir, the Indus and even beyond, so also the provinces beyond the Jumna and the Ganges up to the Kumaon mountains and Badrikeshwar including Bengal and the cities of Kashi, Prayag and Gaya. You have stopped the free conveyance of the imperial treasures from the provinces to the capital. You have taken possession of Chitor, Dwarka and Gujarat, collected tributes from the nearest province of Agra, violated the revered imperial seat of Delhi and disrespected the Emperor's throne, by proclaiming your own regulations during annual incursions. You have projected the conquest of the whole earth together with the four oceans, reaching Roum-Sham itself, whose Emperor Sultan Muhammad* has therefore ordered his son to march across the Indus into India and restore the Mughal Emperor to his traditional honours and position, of which you have deprived him. On this account I have undertaken this distant campaign in order to avenge your enormities, to liberate Delhi and the Emperor, a holy figure deserving respect from Muslims and Hindus alike, who has been betrayed by his faithless servants.

" I therefore enjoin it upon you to leave the Emperor alone, take whatever expenses you have incurred and quietly return to your part of the country. You have been the cause of all the powerful 52 chiefs, like Rana Sang-

*An Emperor of this name reigned at Constantinople from 1730 to 1754.

ram Sinh of Chitor and Udaipur, the Marwar ruler of Ajmere, Savai Jaysinh of Jaypur, withholding payment of their tributes to the Emperor and trying with your aid to turn the whole of India into a land of the Hindus. I have therefore been commanded by my master of Roum Sham to chastise you and all those like you who have dared to show disrespect to the Emperor. It is my mission to pursue you to the bitter end. Even in the six imperial Subahs of Deccen your aggressions have been enormous. You have humbled the Nizam, conquered the old royal seats of Bijapur, Bidar, Daulatabad and Ahmadnagar, subjugated the territory of the Karnatak, fired guns on Hyderabad, taken possession of all the sea-coasts and important cities within them as far as Sondhe, Bednor, Trichinopoly, Srirangapattan, Machhlipatan, Goa, Konkan and Cambay, in addition to the northern cities of Sironj, Bhilsa, and Gadhamandla. Moreover you have by sheer force occupied all the strong and renowned forts and castles and the island fortresses belonging to all these territories. You have brought under subjection, both by deceit and stratagem, the large and fruitful provinces of Khandesh, Nemad, Berar and Khechivada, and have become so bold as to place a Hindu Emperor on the throne of Delhi. You have deprived innumerable tributaries and chiefs, who had paid allegiance to the Emperor, of all their belongings and sent them into exile. Several of them have turned fakirs and beggars.

"I well know how your ancestors defied all the brave and powerful generals deputed by Aurangzeb to check them such as Shaistakhan, Zulphikarkhan, Jaysinh and many others.* You utterly ruined them and their relatives, so that even their names are no more heard. But remember you cannot any longer practise the same tricks with me. I warn you to retire to the south of the river Narmada and rest contented with your possession of the Deccan. If you agree, well and good ; if not you will see the consequences. You are free to make your choice."

---

* A long list of over twenty is given which I have omitted. A few repetitions here and there are also omitted.

7. *Madhavrao, the greatest of the Peshwas*

Peshwa Balajirao left behind him two sons, Madhavrao and Narayanrao, and one brother Raghunathrao. The first was then sixteen years old and succeeded to the Peshwaship as his father's heir. His uncle Raghunathrao had hoped, however, to conduct the administration and strenuously exerted himself to keep Madhavrao permanently in a state of pupilage. But the latter possessed by nature a mature judgment, a high spirit and the talents both of a soldier and a statesman. The initial friction soon grew into open rupture, when the uncle claimed a half share in the raj, an impracticable demand. A civil war ensued and ended in 1768 in a victory for the young Peshwa who captured his uncle and kept him strictly confined in his palace at Poona.

Enemies were not wanting to take advantage of the Maratha disaster at Panipat now aggravated by this domestic dissension. Nizam Ali marched with all speed towards Poona, but was, after a protracted struggle of two years, routed completely at Raksasbhuvan and compelled to submit. The Peshwa at once assumed the supreme control of his Government and thereafter employed Nana Phadnis and Haripant Phadke as the principal Secretaries to execute his orders. The famous Ramshastri whom the Peshwa adored almost as his guru, shed lustre on the working of his Judicial Department.

One indirect result of the disaster of Panipat was the unchecked rise of Hyder Ali in Mysore, who seized the occasion to aggrandize himself in the Karnatak and strove to extinguish all traces of Maratha conquest in that region. Madhavrao had therefore to spend the best part of his time and resources in recapturing all his former territories and exacting complete submission from Hyder Ali. Simultaneously with his Karnatak expeditions, the Peshwa subdued the Bhosles of Nagpur, brought them back to allegiance to the Central Government, and exacted from them terms of an agreement acknowledging the Peshwa as the suzerain of the Maratha State and promising to support him against all rebels and enemies. This treaty of Kankapur in 1769 is known as a master stroke of the young Peshwa's valour and capacity in organizing the united power of the Maratha State.

In the same year the Peshwa despatched a strong expedition under two Brahman and two Maratha commanders to restore the Maratha prestige and claims at the Court of Delhi and in the northern regions in general, which had received a set-back since the day of Panipat. The four leaders, among whom Mahadji Sindia was one, won remarkable success in their undertaking, restored the Emperor to his ancestors' throne at Delhi, humbled the Rohillas, and carried out all the former Maratha commitments usually understood by the term Hindu-pad-Padshahi. Just at the moment when the Maratha arms and diplomacy had reached their culmination, this greatest of the Peshwas succumbed to an inherited tendency to consumption and died in November 1772 at the premature age of 28, to the severe grief of the whole nation. This event has been rightly considered, both then and now, as the greatest misfortune which the Maratha Power sustained since the death of Shivaji.

Says Grant Duff : "Although the military talents of Madhavrao were very considerable, his character as a sovereign is entitled to far higher praise and to much greater respect than that of any of his predecessors. He is deservedly celebrated for his firm support of the weak against the oppressive, of the poor against the rich, and, as far as the constitution of society admitted, for his equity to all." Writes Kincaid : "Madhavrao spent his life in the service of his country. Threatened both by domestic and foreign enemies, he triumphed signally over all. His triumphs brought him no rest ; he spent all his time in tireless labour to relieve the condition of his people. Quick to anger, he was no less quick to forgive. And the only fault that the harshest critic can find in this admirable ruler is that he shortened his life, so precious to his people, by his arduous and unceasing toil."

The sequel is easily told. Madhavrao's younger brother Narayanrao assumed the Peshwaship, when his uncle Raghoba, who was still in confinement, made an effort to escape, thereby bringing down upon himself stricter vigilance from his custodians. His partizans thereupon formed a plot to restore him to power and put the nephew into confinement instead, with the result that the latter was murdered by the guards in an attempt to apprehend him. This atrocious deed excited keen resentment among the nation and was traced to his uncle Raghoba as its prime author upon a full and impartial enquiry by the celebrated Ram Shastree. The responsible ministers and leaders then formed a Council of State known as the *Bara-Bhai* for the conduct of affairs, ousted Raghoba from power, and carried on the government in the name of the newly born son of the murdered Peshwa. The banished Raghoba sought shelter with the British at Surat and with their help tried to regain the Peshwaship, thus leading to a long war which has become famous in Anglo-Indian history.

8. *British jealousy at the increasing Maratha power.*

The third Peshwa Balaji Bajirao by a series of victories both in arms and diplomacy nearly succeeded in making the Maratha power supreme and respected throughout the length and breadth of India. The British had readily helped him in putting down the rebel Angria in 1756, but they soon grew jealous of the Peshwa's supremacy and would not continue their cordial help to him when he undertook, two years later, a campaign for the conquest of Janjira from the Sidi, who was then the only existing menace to Maratha aggression. They had also at this time taken forcible possession of the castle of Surat, considerably damaging thereby the Peshwa's interests in that quarter. If the Marathas succeeded in ousting the Sidi from his possession of Janjira, the British feared that the Maratha arms might next be turned against them and threaten their position at Bombay. Particularly was this the case during the Seven Years' War then raging, when the British and the French were in open hostility in all quarters of the globe. In the midst of this situation the Peshwa got offended at the British refusal to help him against the Sidi in 1758, and was publicy reported to be seeking an alliance with the French, the object being the French conquest of Bombay and the Maratha conquest of Janjira, with mutual co-operation. This turn of events so exercised the minds of the British authorities at Bombay, that with a view to soothing the Peshwa and disarming his antagonism, they sent Mr. Price to Poona as their envoy in September 1759. The envoy was hospitably treated by the Peshwa, who, however, would not enter into any discussion with him on the subject of his mission ; and consequently Mr. Price returned without achieving anything.

Eight years passed, and the next Peshwa Madhavrao succeeded in quickly asserting the Maratha power in all quarters of India. Again, the British got alarmed and hearing of the growing estrangement between the Peshwa and his uncle sent their agent Mr. Mostyn to Poona in 1767 and another agent Mr. Broome to the uncle Raghoba at Nasik, 'in order to check the growing power of the Marathas as much as possible.' Raghoba bitterly complained to Mr. Broome of the ingratitude of his nephew and requested British help to put him down. But as Raghoba would not offer any specific advantages in lieu of British help, the negotiations proved barren of results. Mr. Mostyn's mission to the Peshwa at Poona gained no better success. Four years later, however, the Peshwa received Mr. Mostyn again as a British envoy at Poona, but when accordingly he reached the place, the Peshwa was in the grip of his last malady and died two months after, in November 1772. Mr. Mostyn, however, continued to reside at Poona for some years, reporting to Bombay the events at the Maratha Court, consequent on the murder of Peshwa Narayanrao. The British at the suggestion of Mostyn sheltered the fugitive Raghoba at Surat and thereby started a war with the Marathas which lasted for seven years and is known as the First Maratha War in Anglo-Indian history.

LECTURE VI

MAHADJI SINDIA AND NANA PHADNIS

1. *Three periods of Maratha history.*

Two men escaped with their lives, under providential guidance, from the fateful field of Panipat, and having soon after risen to exceptional prominence by dint of personal ability and character, became the saviours of the Maratha kingdom almost up to the time of its downfall by the Treaty of Bassein. The Maratha kingdom formally ended in the year 1818 : but virtually it lost its independence with the Treaty of Bassein, (1802), by which Baji Rao II as the head of the Maratha State, accepted British supremacy and might perhaps have retained his subordinate position at the capital of Poona, on a par with the present Maharajas of Gwalior, Indore or Baroda, had he possessed the necessary wisdom to steer clear of the difficulties that afterwards arose and to submit willingly and cheerfully to the British overlordship as the others did. We must therefore put down the end of the Maratha kingdom on the last day of the Christian year 1802, and sub-divide our subject accordingly. If I may calculate Shivaji's beginning of Maratha Swaraj somewhere from the middle of the 17th century, say 1653,* the period of the first sixty years up to 1713 when the Peshwas' regime started, has on it a clear stamp of Shivaji's personality and has already been shown to be distinct in character from the next sixty years, 1713 to 1773, when the Maratha power reached its highest expansion due to the exceptional capacity of the first four Peshwas and when the Saranjami system involving feudal military service had its full force. Thereafter comes the period of decline extend-

* In a letter dated 17 July 1653 Shivaji declares that his *swarajya* is an accomplished fact.—Patrasarsangraha No. 642.

ing over thirty years dating from the murder of Peshwa Narayan Rao in 1773 and ending, as I have said, with the Treaty of Bassein in 1802, thus making a total existence of 150 years for the Maratha dominion in India. This last period of 30 years bears a distinct stamp of the two personalities, Balaji Janardan *alias* Nana Phadnis and Mahadji Sindia, of whom I am now going to speak.

There exists a great deal of misconception about the intentions and achievements of these two contemporary characters, not only outside Maharastra but even within it, as the subject, I am afraid, has not hitherto been treated in a proper historical spirit by making use of all the available papers and information. I think it would not be out of place here to give my estimate of them and their work, and with it also an account of the declining stage of Maratha politics, leading logically to my next discourse on the causes of the Maratha downfall. In this way, taking into consideration the division into the three periods mentioned above, I shall have cursorily explained the main characteristics of them all from the beginning. Nana and Mahadji, the one a Brahman and pure statesman, the other a Maratha and soldier-statesman, were often helpmates, occasionally rivals for power, but both always intensely watchful about the national interests.

2. *Early careers of Mahadji and Nana.*

Mahadji was born about the year 1727 and was therefore 67 years of age at his death in 1794. Nana was 14 years younger, having been born in 1741. Both had full opportunity to observe and study closely the development of Maratha concerns under Peshwa Balaji Rao, and both received much of their initial training under him and rendered conspicuous service to Madhav Rao, to whom they entirely owed their rise and future career and who was able to maintain his position against his uncle mainly through their loyal support. From the beginning Nana and Mahadji were opposed to the policy and ways of Raghoba, who would have sacked them both at any time, if he had the power to do it. It is well known that when the question of succession to Sindia's estate came up for consideration after the disaster of Panipat, where three valiant representatives of that family had lost their lives, Raghoba set aside the claim of Mahadji and appointed one Manaji Sindia known as *Phakde,* a distant relation. But Madhav Rao felt the injustice of this measure, since Mahadji was the only surviving member of Ranoji's large and devoted family and fully deserved to succeed to the estate as the direct heir, even though he was an illegitimate son of his father. After Manaji had enjoyed the position for two years, Mahadji was reinstated by Madhav Rao and naturally felt ever after a great aversion for Raghoba, whom he considered utterly incompetent. Similarly was Nana Phadnis a confidant of Peshwa Madhav Rao who employed him specially to watch and superintend the wily Raghoba, when he was put in confinement after the battle of Dhodap in 1768. Nana had, therefore, to incur the highest displeasure of Raghoba from the beginning. This tension grew into an open rupture after the murder of Narayan Rao, when Nana and Sakharam Bapu formed the great league against the murderer. Their object was to set aside Raghoba and conduct the administration, first in the name of Narayan Rao's widow Ganga Bai, and afterwards on behalf of her newly born son known as Savai Madhav Rao. During the twenty years from the birth of this Peshwa in 1774 to 1794, there was a minority adminisstration, which gave Nana and Mahadji the opportunity to prove their ability. They discharged their duty, as we know, with conspicuous success.

The careers of Nana and Mahadji are divided into two main periods by the course of events, the first from 1774 to 1783 known as the first Maratha War, and the second 1784-94 when Mahadji, openly giving up the old guerilla tactics, raised a new army on the European model under the direction of De Boigne,—the greatest European adventurer in India, having experience of two European wars,—conquered the Rajput princes, captured Delhi, and took the Emperor under his protection after rescuing him from the ignominious atrocities inflicted upon him by Ghulam Qadir. Thus Mahadji attained a high importance and an eminent position in the whole of India, when he returned to Poona with pomp and honours lying thick upon his head, but unfortunately, only to die in his native land shortly after. Nana and Mahadji are the two personalities who preserved the Maratha power after the murder of Narayan Rao, when Raghoba took the help of the British.

Those who have studied the contemporary European history and watched closely the career of Warren Hastings in India, can at once realize how this first Maratha War, synchronizing with the War of American Independence, was affected by foreign politics, since the French navy for a time regained its lost influence and caused serious anxiety to the British in their world-wide antagonism. As we know, British ambition began to bid for world power in 1756 in the Seven Years' War, at the end of which they established their naval supremacy by the Treaty of Paris in 1763. The next ten years was a period of arrested ambition for them, which was rekindled by the murder of the Peshwa at Poona, of which they took full advantage by their wanton aggression in capturing the fort of Thana from the Peshwa's possession at the end of 1774. Next year Nelson visited Bombay, although he was then quite an unknown personality, looking for naval expansion in eastern waters and possibly imparting part of his zeal to Warren Hastings and other British officials in India. But during the War of American Independence British ambition received a set-back in all quarters of the globe. The French fleet had become superior to the British for a short time.

In order to obtain a proper grasp of Maratha history of this period, the student must keep before his mind's eye the international character of British politics ; and the following lines from Sir Alfred Lyall make it clear how Nana and Mahadji saved Maratha independence at this great crisis : " In 1776 a turn of European politics materially affected the situation in India. A French agent reached Poona in 1777, proposing alliance with the Marathas and promising them French help against the English.' The Marathas were then and up to nearly the end of the century a match for the English. By the summer of 1780 the fortunes of the English in India had fallen to their lowest watermark. The Marathas were too well-united to be shaken. They held in the centre of India a position which enabled them to threaten all the three divided English Presidencies. The backing given by the English to Raghunathrao turned out a disastrous speculation and ended in ignominious failure. Hyder Ali made common cause with the Marathas and drew the Nizam into the triple alliance which Nana Phadnis had formed against the English. Sindia was fast becoming the most powerful chief of the Maratha Federation. Next year a large French fleet arrived in India under Admiral Suffren than whom France has never had a better admiral. The situation was saved for the English by news arriving of peace between England and France and the troublesome Maratha War ended, during which the English power in India underwent some perilous vicissitudes."

3. *How the two leaders won the First Maratha War*

In the year 1773, of which we are now speaking, the Regulating Act brought all the British Presidencies of India under one united control at Calcutta. Warren Hastings was appointed Governor-General with a council of four members to help him. There occurred open disagreement between them which not a little affected the fortunes of the Marathas. On that account the course of events during the period has become so confused and complicated, that it requires careful study from original materials, both English and Marathi, in order to determine the exact position of Indian affairs and preserve a proper mental perspective. Had not Nana and Mahadji acted in concert and brought all their resources to bear on this war with the British, there would have been an end of the Maratha power at this juncture. The British had not even a plausible excuse at the time for giving shelter to Raghoba, and starting a wanton war, after an heir had been born to the murdered Peshwa. The British should have treated Raghoba as a fugitive and murderer and given him no shelter. They, however, sustained a set-back in America by the loss of their colonies, and had their prestige lowered in their dealings with France. Warren Hastings, by his ambition and aggression, estranged the minds of very many chiefs and potentates of India. The Emperor would not trust himself to the British ; the Nawab of Oudh and the Raja of Benares had no better opinion of their veracity. The Nizam in the east and Hyder in the south, the Marathas in the west and the Bhosles of Nagpur in the centre, signed a solemn secret treaty of alliance for a joint war against the British. French proposals of naval and military help were, as has been mentioned above, openly entertained at Poona, so that Nana's sagacity and foresight made matters so adverse to the British interests, that orders came from Europe for Warren Hastings to stop all wars and restore peaceful relations with the various Powers in India. The Treaty of Salbye, first proposed in the autumn of 1781 and ultimately ratified in February 1783, restored peace to India, and freed Maratha arms for completing their previous commitments. This organization of national forces at a critical moment of the country's fortunes and the preservation of Maratha independence from the British aggression, have been set down as the greatest achievements of Nana Phadnis, at whose death in 1800 it was universally felt, that all moderation and wisdom vanished from Maratha politics, leaving the field free for the foundation of British supremacy in India.

Mahadji Sindia's services to the Maratha nation are of a different type. His greatest achievements have been put down to be his conquest of the Rajputs, his settlement of the Emperor's affairs, and the creation of armaments on the western scientific method. The valuable experience he had obtained during seven years of incessant warfare, convinced him, that the future enemy of the Maratha nation was to be a western power and that therefore unless they changed their traditional fighting methods, they had no hope of life. He had at the same time to carry out the old Maratha policy of controlling the Emperor's affairs at Delhi and re-establishing Maratha supremacy over the Rajput and other tributary States, which had thrown off their former allegiance during the war with the British. These three tasks occupied Mahadji during the rest of his life for twelve years and at times even brought him to the brink of ruin.

I shall discuss later, why, with all this glowing expansion and success of Maratha arms in all quarters of India, that Power crumbled so easily in the early years of the 19th century. But the seeds of that ultimate decay were, as will be shown in the sequel, more or less sown in the midst of this apparent glory and during the regime of this last politician Nana Phadnis. It is a matter of common knowledge that there ever existed a kind of irritation and rivalry between Nana and Mahadji, the origin and nature of which, we must carefully study.

4. *Physical and temperamental differences between the two.*

Since Nana and Mahadji are practically responsible for having made the Maratha history of the last quarter of the 18th century and since they often worked jointly and oftener disagreed also, I think it necessary to probe their character, achievements and failures a little more deeply. The two differed from each other as much in their physical features as in their mental cast. Nana, a Brahman, tall and thin, brownish in complexion with a long oval face, marked with large piercing eyes and a long nose; the other a Kshatriya, of middle stature, dark, thickset, stout and athletic, a typical Maratha soldier of his time. While Nana was by nature strict and serious, regular and hard working, abstemious in words and action, difficult of approach and never given to sport, mirth or company, hardly ever seen to laugh and of an extremely delicate and thin constitution; Mahadji was, on the other hand, of a jovial and merry temperament, ever surrounded by crowds of people, talking, joking, laughing and enjoying company, taking counsel with all, but always so cautious as to set people entirely on a wrong scent, never to let others fathom his real intentions or plans; in fact, an exact antithesis of Nana. Mahadji is described as sitting in a large tent in the midst of clerks and servants, helpmates and ambassadors, questioning all openly, hearing and dictating correspondence and issuing orders simultaneously. Nana has often taken Mahadji to task for not keeping his counsels secret and for discussing important State matters in an open assembly. People, including even his near relatives and immediate servants, were afraid of approaching Nana. He was exacting and strict in his punishments, would see and talk to only one person at a time, except rarely when there was an open discussion or conference previously arranged. Even Haripant Phadke, Nana's best friend, would consult the latter's whim before he approached him with any proposal or suggestion. In one particular point of common occurrence, the contrast between Nana and Mahadji was most vivid. Under the greatest of disasters, Mahadji was cool and composed, never showing his innermost trepidation to anybody. When the news of severe reverses or decimation of his large forces reached him, he could be seen laughing and joking as usual, as if nothing had happened. This unperturbed intrepidity and cool decision carried him successfully through trials and embarrassments which would break the spirit of any ordinary man. Nana was timorous and excitable., often unable to conceal his confusion when difficult problems demanded immediate solution. First Sakharam Bapu, and later Haripant Phadke always helped to compose Nana's disturbed temperament and hearten him in the midst of perilous situations. But, unlike Mahadji, Nana was usually reasonable and fair in his dealings, afraid to commit treachery or wrong, strict and punctual in carrying out his word, not over-inclined to liberality and as a rule impatient of results. He did not possess the self-sufficiency of Mahadji, but took counsel with all separately and acted according to a considered judgment of his own. Mahadji on the other hand was patient and courageous, brilliant under reverses, shifting and calculating, often irascible in temper, ever inclined to pick up the weaknesses of others and make the best use of them, as we know from his dealings with Nana, Raghoba, Sakharam Bapu, or Tukoji and Ahalya Bai Holkar. He showed a friendly spirit to all, but would not be over-scrupulous in keeping his word or doing a wrong act if it suited his purpose.

He can be called a great statesman, in whom even his enemies could put their faith. Lacking the generous heart of Balaji Rao or Madhav Rao, Nana Phadnis was not at all loved like them. Being a stern taskmaster, he could hardly expect love from others ; nay, he was often in danger of assassination and has himself mentioned some twenty occasions on which he had a miraculous escape from attempts on his life, which never was the case with any of the Peshwas before. Nana's rigorous system of spying often made it impossible for him to distinguish between friends and foes, so that his own trusted servants like Ghasiram Kotwal or Balwant Rao Nagnath who possessed his confidence, did not scruple to gain their own selfish ends. Indeed the atmosphere of Poona for the eight or ten years after Narayan Rao's murder, remained intensely surcharged with uncertainty and suspicion to a degree quite unbearable even to those who had no concern with State affairs. Life and property were felt to be quite insecure.

Nana lacked military leadership, while Mahadji lacked the aptitude for desk-work or for accounts and attention to details, matters in which Nana was a master hand. In fact the records of Nana Phadnis had to be so methodically arranged in his days that they showed his inexhaustible capacity for labour and precision. A long mutilated paper extant in Nana's own hand has been printed in the *K. S. Patren Yadi*, which contains half-finished directions and arrangements, relating to the grand ceremony of the young Peshwa's marriage in February 1783 and which shows how careful Nana was of the minutest detail, as he mentions, for instance, numerous courses and articles of food that were to be got ready for each day and for different occasions, with minute instructions how they should be arranged and served. Mahadji was not so exact, and was often cheated by unscrupulous subordinates and employees, whom he then visited with relentless vengeance. These differences although only temperamental in the beginning, became accentuated later on and for a time affected Maratha politics throughout India. Nana was strong in statesmanship and Mahadji in military matters ; when they acted in mutual concert and enjoyed each other's confidence, they produced the greatest effect ; but they often felt jealous of each other and pursued independent courses thereby affecting the Maratha fortunes adversely. Nana confined his attention mostly to the south, Mahadji to the north. They did not meet for over 10 years and had no personal exchange of views. They corresponded frequently, but after all, written correspondence, which often evoked acrimonious, wordy and endless explanations, could not settle all the growing concerns of a vast and scattered State, and resulted in irritation and discomfiture for all workers. Hundreds of letters and papers have been printed, out of the correspondence that passed between various persons and parties during the 20 years in which these two men, as the principal actors on the stage, conducted the Maratha affairs : they clearly show the contrast to which I have alluded above.

5. *Drawbacks of Nana's policy.*

The personal contrast having thus been made clear, I shall now proceed to discuss what I consider to be the drawbacks of Nana's policy.

(*a*) WANT OF CONCILIATORY SPIRIT.

Nana started his work as a member of the ministerial Cabinet called the Council of the *Bara-Bhais* or 'Twelve Brothers,' of which at the beginning the veteran Sakharam Bapu was the sole moving spirit. Nana's cousin Moroba, Trimbakrao Pethe, Haripant Phadke, Mahadji Sindia, Tukoji Holkar, Bhavanrao Pratinidhi, Maloji Ghorpade, in fact most of the prominent persons of the day, were supposed to be members of this Council, which would have been strong and capable of lasting results, had it continued on the lines on which it was started. Perhaps instead of Nana's personal rule, the nation would have more readily submitted to the rule of a strong and wise cabinet. It was indeed a singular opportunity for working out a constitutional system of government in the place of the personal rule of a dictator. Nana shows full knowledge of the working of Hastings' Council at Calcutta and of Hornby's Council at Bombay, where matters were decided on the principle of the majority of votes. Both the Chhatrapati and the Peshwa had proved failures, so that Nana's past experience and foresight should have convinced him of the wisdom of continuing the *Bara-Bhai* Council for the Maratha administration. Instead of taking this line, instead of replacing incompetent members by those in his own confidence, he gradually removed all the members, one by one, and concentrated all power in his own hand. Sakharam Bapu and Moroba Phadnis, two of his best colleagues, were removed and imprisoned on a charge of treason. Imbued with a conciliatory spirit so very essential for such concerns, Sakharam Bapu was often compelled by circumstances to have separate dealings with all parties, with even enemies during war time, *e.g.* with Raghoba, the Nizam, Hyder Ali and the British. Nana looked upon this as double-dealing or treason, and got him imprisoned. If it was necessary to remove both Bapu and Maroba, he should at least have introduced new members to take their places, but after a couple of years even the name of the *Bara-Bhais* is not seen to exist. Treason in those days had a peculiar meaning. Narayan Rao was murdered, certainly at the instigation of Raghoba, who was however the only surviving member of the Peshwas' family, and for whose past services, with all his faults, very many people felt a sort of reverence. Except a few implacable spirits who were determined to visit the late Peshwa's murderers with severe punishment, there was a large body of public opinion in Maharastra, which looked at the event more leniently and advocated a conciliatory policy. Many were indifferent whether Raghoba or the new born baby ruled their destinies ; they certainly wished that Raghoba should be provided with means of decent comfort commensurate with his position. Left to his own resources, and reckless of consequences, Raghoba seduced sardars and formed a strong party of his own, particularly winning over those who in previous times had served him faithfully. In these circumstances Sakaram Bapu tried his best to stop the disastrous war and restore the normal administration by a policy of compromise, avoiding extreme measures towards the recalcitrant Raghoba, Mahadji Sindia and others and even Sakharam Bapu did not view with favour the adoption of severe measures against Raghoba. These men, therefore, appeared to Nana as traitors deserving punishment. In the case of Mahadji, Nana was helpless, otherwise, if he had the means, he would have punished him in the same way as he did Sakharam Bapu. This obviously amounts to a mistake of statesmanship on the part of Nana. Forgiveness in such cases forms a part of practical wisdom. But Nana was inexorable in his methods of punishment. When a son was born to Narayan Rao, Raghoba lost his pretensions and should have been allowed to run away as a fugitive. He was however, tenaciously pursued and unwillingly driven into the arms of the British, which brought about the war, all but shattering the prestige of the Marathas. It was enough to take the wind out of Raghoba's sails as the Queen's Proclamation did in the case of the mutineers of 1857. If the *Bara-Bhais* had issued a proclamation asking people to come back to their avocations and warning them against sympathizing with the fugitive Raghoba, matters would probably have settled down quietly and Raghoba would have obtained no support outside. Many sardars and influential leaders acted only as the exigencies of the moment required, looking to their own personal interest, and siding with the party which benefited them most. Nana on the other hand by means of close spying obtained full details of each and every follower of Raghoba, confiscated properties and houses, and punished their families and relations, which terribly exasperated the people for many years, so that the functions of a normal administration were almost brought to a standstill. The conciliatory policy pursued by Bapu would perhaps have availed better. It would have restored amity in the Peshwa's family, left no permanent scars and sores behind. Baji Rao II. might possibly have grown up with a different attitude not only towards Nana but all others upon whom he later on tried to wreak his vengeance. This aspect of Nana's policy deserves to be noted by students of history.

(*b*) DID NOT REALIZE BRITISH PRESSURE IN THE NORTH.

Nana was much irritated at the prominence which Mahadji attained in the conduct of the Treaty of Salbye. He could not understand why Mahadji withdrew to the north and established himself far away in Malwa, leaving the conduct of the Deccan campaign to others. Not conversant with military affairs, Nana could not realize that the centre of gravity of Indian politics was fast shifting from the Deccan to the north. Clever as Nana was in acquiring through his agents and spies the minutest information and details of movements and events that happened hundreds of miles away, he could not realize the heavy military pressure which the rising British power was bringing to bear upon the future of India, from the east and the north, where they slowly consolidated their position so as to make a further move and circumvent the Maratha power when a suitable opportunity would arise. Of all Indians Mahadji alone understood this pressure from personal and practical experience of the military dispositions of the British. Nana was ever insistent in calling Mahadji to the south in order not only to fight the national enemies in the Deccan, but mainly to control any independent move on his part. Mahadji had closely watched the celebrated victorious march of General Goddard from the river Jumna to Burhanpur and on to Surat, splitting the whole of north India as it were into halves like a piece of bamboo. The havoc which the British guns had made during the campaign of Talegaum and the ease with which the British were quietly strengthening their position on the west coast by the capture of Bassein and Thana, were factors which impressed Mahadji immensely. To effect a counterpoise, he withdrew himself entirely from the south, knowing that he could get the best terms in his contemplated move for peace with the British, if he could deal with them in the north rather than at the Court of Poona, where the pressure from the Bombay Government was irresistible. From the ample correspondence that is now available on the subject, Mahadji seems to have urged that if he had withdrawn his troops into the south, the British would have captured Central India by one stroke, taken possession of the Emperor and dictated terms to the Marathas at Poona. Such a catastrophe to Maratha fortunes, which Mahadji wanted to prevent, was inexplicable to Nana, who ever after suspected treason on Mahadji's part against the central Maratha Government in every plan or move that Mahadji undertook or suggested, and, Nana gave open directions to his agents to thwart Mahadji, who, on the other hand followed a conciliatory policy towards Warren Hastings and did his best indirectly to frustrate the English designs in Bengal, Oudh, Central India and Delhi, for which he had to station himself for a long time between Mathura and Gwalior, in order to exercise a direct and immediate check. In fact, it certainly becomes clear that Nana did not understand the situation in the north, nor realize that no amount of clever diplomacy is so effective as when it is backed by the sword. He should have done well to go there personally and share with Mahadji the risks and responsibilities involved in the long drawn struggle. But suspicious by nature, Nana was always afraid of his life, and would not easily venture into Mahadji's camp.

Maratha politics at that time would have attained immense strength if Nana had taken the young Peshwa to the north, and putting his own personality in the background, allowed a free hand to Mahadji. The promising young Peshwa would have received a valuable preparation for his future career, had he been allowed to visit the northern regions about the year 1787 or 88, when he was fourteen years of age. All the persons in the Peshwas' family started active life about the age of twelve and such practical experience was the most healthy and necessary equipment for the nation upon which the Maratha Raj was built up. Nana should have allowed the outside world to see that a young master was growing in the Peshwas' house, so that petty internal jealousies and the spirit of insubordination, which had been so rampant, would have been kept under check. Many irritating problems and important political topics, such as the disputes between Mahadji and Ali Bahadur, the war with Tipu, the disordered affairs of the Holkars, to name only a few among a host of others, could have been easily settled on the spot in personal discussion and compromise. Several misunderstandings between Nana and Mahadji themselves, which now form volumes of printed records, would have been directly cleared. But Nana's suspicious nature and fear of danger to his life, prevented the Peshwa from undertaking any journey beyond about a hundred miles radius from Poona. Wai and Nasik are about the only places that the Peshwa had visited, before he died at the age of twenty-one. Even a visit to Bombay, which the British so cordially suggested would have been most educative. But the solicitude of Nana for the young Peshwa's life was too strong to permit him to obtain the sort of education he most needed. In view of the Peshwa's premature death, however, such a discussion seems now out of place.

6. *Confused affairs of Mahadji*

In criticizing Nana Phadnis' administration let me not create a wrong impression about the inherent ability of Mahadji Sindia either. For, as I have more than once remarked, he too was not free from blame for mismanagement and irregularities which seem to be ingrained in the nature of the Marathas. Here is a typical instance corroborated by contemporary evidence, showing how Mahadji's affairs were in great disorder and confusion. One Sadashiv

Dinkar, an agent of Nana Phadnis, sent the following pertinent observations to him at Poona, from the camp of Mahadji Sindia near Mathura about the year 1788 :

"A regular income, a fixed expenditure and moderation are the three essentials of any sound undertaking. Mahadji has just obtained ten lacs, but you will be surprised to learn how the money has been spent. As for his army expenditure, the Maratha forces from the Deccan have been suffering appalling miseries which I am unable to describe in words. They are not able to pay off their debts even by selling their horses. A trooper hardly gets Rs. 10 a month ; how can he live on this? Mahadji has spent tremendously on his new regiments of infantry, but his eminent Maratha assistants, who laid their lives down in capturing Gohad and Gwalior, have suffered terrible destitution. Mahadji never enquires if all the men put down on paper in the roll of the infantry regiments are really present or not. There is no inspection, no roll-call and the vast amounts spent on them do not reach the hands of the men to whom they are due, but the money is pocketed by unscrupulous middlemen. There is enormous confusion and misappropriation. The artillery also is entirely mismanaged. All the employees from the Deccan have left service and returned home. Money has been poured into useless channels. I have already said how scanty the income of Mahadji is. Then come the huge sums borrowed from the bankers who are demanding payment. Abaji Naik demands thirty lacs. There is any number of other money-lenders, Deccani, Hindu, Gujarati, Rangde (Marwadis), whose demands for repayment are pressing, and who have been worrying Mahadji severely. He has already mortgaged the prospective income of the next two years. He has exhausted all his private purse also, which was reported to contain some twenty-five lacs. Excessive rains during the last four years have reduced the country to a condition of famine. One of Mahadji's revenue collectors had to resort to inhuman measures in order to squeeze money out of the cultivators. He tied rags to the bodies of the rich and the poor alike and pouring oil on them set them on fire. You can easily imagine the state of the country under such hardships. Lands have been deserted, cultivation has stopped ; what little was produced was taken away by the old claimants, predecessors of Mahadji. Owing to famine some villages have become depopulated ; one house has been found to contain twenty dead bodies with no one alive in it to dispose of them : such is the case of the country between the Chambal and Kashmir. Dense crowds of men are seen streaming from one place to another in search of food. Famine and robbery have enhanced their agony, and a third evil, *viz.* Mahadji's tax-collectors, has now been added to the first two, for these collectors are by no means less exacting ; but with all their efforts they could hardly collect any cash. As regards tribute from the various States, Jaypur agreed on paper to pay twenty-one lacs : a large amount it looks, but only two lacs were paid in cash and two more in jewellery by slow degrees ; the remainder, it was stipulated was to be collected from the ryots of the State, and for that purpose 2000 troops have been despatched into Jaypur territory. This is the condition of one State only. There are others who do not come to terms at all. Mahadji has to defray all the expenses of the Emperor and his armies, out of his own pocket. He has borrowed as much as he could get, and has already spent all that he had saved. He alone knows if he has any more cash now in his possession ; he farms out the revenue to the highest bidder ; no Deccani is willing to undertake this farming. Mahadji is in search of a banker who would undertake to pay the Emperor every month out of the collections farmed out to him. The present bankers being all helpless, refuse to undertake this impracticable job. I know what I am writing ; it is the naked truth. A healthy administration is that in which the master is never in want and in which the army is contented, and the ryots are happy. If these three conditions do not exist, God alone can take care of them. His will must prevail."

If this was the condition of the finances of one

of our best and the most famous chiefs in his palmy days, we can easily imagine what Maratha rule was like in its declining period. As I have said, things were different during the 60 years regime of the first four Peshwas. The above description only shows that matters were drifting towards a rapid fall.

As regards the charge that Mahadji was trying to gain independence to serve his own ends, so as to injure the interests of the Maratha State, I have not been able to find any evidence to sustain it. He perhaps claimed a free hand in the management of affairs, when he was convinced that the State was going to ruin. He never discarded the help or association of Nana, whose capacity no one else knew better. One thing is quite clear. Mahadji has again and again expressed his unbounded confidence in the devotion and sagacity of Nana, whose agent Sadashiv Dinkar gives the following account of his interview with Mahadji in September 1788 : " It gives me supreme pleasure to inform you, that just as a drowning man recovers courage upon learning that some one is coming to his rescue, so did Mahadji feel immense relief from his critical position in the midst of enemies when timely help of money and forces came under Ali Bahadur from the Deccan. Mahadji frankly confesses, to the shame of his numerous dependents, that in his sore need no one ran to his help as did his noble brother Nana. Great are those who do great things."

7. *Limitations of Nana's power*

It was a mere grievous accident, I mean the murder of Narayan Rao, that brought Nana to the front. He was quite aware of his own weakness, *viz.*, that he was not a general and never could lead armies on a battlefield. For this he had to depend upon others such as Mahadji Sindia, Tukoji Holkar, Haripant Phadke, or Parshuram Bhau Patwardhan. The weakness of such a position particularly in those days can very well be imagined. Of these men Nana found Mahadji alone intractable, so that whenever Mahadji did not readily fall in with Nana's views or policy, there naturally arose a friction, which resulted in strong factions involving prominent persons, and which injured the interests of the State. In such circumstances Mahadji was not the man who would scruple to make the best use of the situation to suit his policy or interest. This sort of factious spirit prevailed throughout the period of their joint careers of 20 years and unconsciously damaged Maratha power and prestige, a result which, in my opinion, would have been averted if Nana had in some cases put his own personality in the background. It is a mistake very common with powerful statesmen, who have already rendered useful services, that they come to think themselves indispensable for the conduct of national affairs, and try to stick to their office when perhaps their retirement might be more advantageous to the public interest. This is particularly the case in eastern politics, where there are no constitutional safeguards as in the British parliamentary system. We can vividly realize this point to-day, if we remember how quietly and easily Prime Ministers of England like Asquith, Lloyd George or MacDonald laid down their own office the moment they found that they had not the nation's support behind them. Nana Phadnis does not seem to have realized the limitations of his own power and usefulness. Particularly is this the case after the unfortunate and untimely death of the young Peshwa in 1795, when Nana, out of love of power, submitted to the crafty Peshwa Baji Rao II., his hereditary enemy, and accepted office under him. If Nana had then quietly withdrawn from politics and watched the situation from a distance, he would possibly have rendered greater service, at least saved himself from humiliation at the hands of worthless intriguers. Nana should have known very well that he was not immortal, that however capable he might have been, his end must come one day, when the nation would have to do without him.

Another point which in my opinion Nana does not seem to have realized, is the reason why most of the old sardars and ministers hesitated to render obedience to him and to execute his orders. Nana was in his original position only a *Phadnis*, a mere head-accountant of the State, much lower in the scale of service than the sardars themselves. He was doubtless acting in the name of the Peshwa who was a child. The sardars had a natural sympathy for the old and experienced Raghoba more than for the little baby in whose name Nana acted. Nana had occasion to understand what a difference there was between the prestige of the Chhatrapati and that of the Peshwas after the death of Shahu. Far less then was his own prestige, when, after the murder of Narayan Rao, power came into his hands. Prestige is of course a nebulous substance having no material value. But prestige often stirs the hearts of men in practical life. Even the strong British Government to-day is very careful about it. In this lies the explanation of the factious and defiant spirit which Nana had to encounter in most of his measures, from his own compatriots.

Nana tried his utmost to bring up the young Peshwa most carefully, and staked his all, even the constitution, upon that one individual, but he should have seen that with all one's efforts it is not humanly possible to make a soldier or a statesman out of a young boy at one's will. Why should Nana think that a youth of 20 could be so trained or trusted as to exercise the full functions of the master of a State and to look after its concerns which he knew were beyond his own capacity? As a matter of fact the young Peshwa, as we know from the ample evidence that is available, would not have proved worthy of his illustrious ancestors, and possibly been no better than Baji Rao II., who so recklessly gambled away the Maratha Raj. Many writers have lamented the untimely death of this young prince, in whom all the nation's hopes were centred, and whom the people had all along fondly hailed as the saviour of the nation, simply because his birth at a critical moment in the nation's fortunes, had saved the realm from the tyranny of the reprobate Raghoba. We now wrongly attribute to his untimely death the eventual fall of the Maratha power.

If this youth had lived long a legitimate master would certainly have been provided, but perhaps by no means a capable one. But more essential was the provision of protective military measures against many of these problems, as the fate of nations is ultimately decided by a recourse to arms. It was therefore the duty of Nana to have followed up Mahadji's measures for the adoption of western military methods. He should have started the same reform of the army in the Deccan in collaboration with Mahadji, instead of suspiciously wrangling over the wording of the terms of the Treaty of Salbye. Failure to improve the military engine of the State detracts much from the sagacity and foresight with which Nana is usually credited. No amount of financial skill, diplomatic wisdom or careful bringing up of the young Peshwa could compensate for this grand failure. The Saranjamdars would doubtless have revolted against a compulsory reform of the old accepted methods, but Nana in co-operation with Mahadji could have carried the same policy through, beginning with his own Huzrat (household cavalry) under Haripant Phadke; the Patwardhans and other sardars could then gradually have been brought into the system. This was the only way of saving the Maratha State.

8. *What could have been done for future safety?*

The Marathas as a race often seem to lack vision and foresight, which is usually seen associated with the Anglo-Sáxon race. Indeed, we marvel at the slow but steady progress of the British nation in the work of empire-building in India. Every step they take is sure, though sometimes slow : if an ambitious spirit like a Wellesley or a Dalhousie follows a vigorous policy, a successor is deliberately selected to soften its rigour and slowly to consolidate the former gains, without having recourse to a retrograde step or a slide back. They never do a single thing without full consultation, discussion and deliberation, in which personalities do not count, and which point only to the ulterior national interests. With us, on the other hand, it is the personalities that count. We neglect to take a long vision and to provide for ultimate objects. We only look to our own immediate concerns of the moment. "When I am gone, the world is nothing to me." is an Indian proverb which aptly illustrates our attitude of mind. When, therefore, we examine the career of Nana Phadnis and join in the chorus of his praise, we do not stop to think what steps he should have taken but did not take, for preserving the Maratha State after him.

The year 1792-93 provided a fit occasion for some such measures being adopted. Mahadji had returned from the north to Poona in June 1792, laden with honours and riches. A grand ceremony was held at Poona for the Peshwa to assume the titles conferred upon him by the Emperor. A campaign against Tipu had given the Marathas a grand success, which had increased their prestige. For nearly two years after this, all the important statesmen and commanders were assembled in Poona under the auspices of the young and rising Peshwa, with high national aspirations, and there were rejoicings for the success in war and diplomacy throughout India, as has been graphically described by Govindrao Kale.* The *holi* festival of March 1793 was performed in Poona with unsurpassed gaiety which has hardly yet died out of the Maratha memory, when, it is said the roads of the city for five miles between the Peshwa's palace and Sindia's camp at Wanodi, were covered with knee-deep coloured powder called *gulal.* These happenings ought to have awakened thoughts about the future in the mind of every sane person. In fact, many in and out of office knew very well that all was not well at home ; that the Chhatraptai was sorely discontented and entertained a secret hatred for the Peshwas : that the Rajputs had been entirely disaffected by the measures of Mahadji ; that the two great figures of the day, Nana and Mahadji, were in open rivalry for power and mastery over the young Peshwa ; that this prince was already showing enough signs of impatience and incapacity to manage the State. Many observant per-

* See P. 15

sons, friends and foes, had sounded enough warnings of the coming danger. If all the wise persons had sat and conferred together on measures of future safety, Nana and Mahadji could have restored the Chhatrapati to power and under his presidency a sort of a new Maratha cabinet or council of management could have been formed. If they had thus acted in a concerted manner and established a kind of regency for the conduct of affairs, some of the future dangers could have been avoided. The scheming family of Raghoba were alive ; his two growing sons were by no means innocuous, as Nana well knew, and could not be done away with ; so some measure was badly needed for protection all round.

From the military point of view the armies of Sindia, Holkar and the Bhosles of Nagpur, all trained under European command, could have been organized and united, as was feared by British observers of the day. But nothing of the kind was done. Such a step was quite possible for Nana, Mahadji and the rest to take, but the minds of these wiseacres do not seem to have peeped into the future. During the next few years death played havoc in the Maratha State, which to some extent contributed to hasten its ultimate downfall. If some urgent measures for future safety had been taken in time, it would have been possible to save the situation. Much of the blame for this neglect ought naturally to go to Nana Phadnis, the last of the Maratha statesmen and head of the Maratha State, handling its affairs for 26 years, An opportune moment presented itself for such a move at the death of the young Peshwa. But personal jealousies rather than concerted action then came into prominence.

These are some of the points which have occurred to me as I read the papers and correspondence of those days and tried to analyse for myself the ultimate cause of the Maratha decline and the workings of the minds of some of the men in authority at the time. There is another charge which some writers have urged against Nana, *viz.*, that of inflating his private purse at the expense of the State. This sort of corruption in public matters was so common in those days, that we need not single out one particular person for blame ; but it is said that Nana's private property amounted to several crores, quite beyond his own needs it would seem. It passes our comprehension how a great financier like him could think his property secure, when his opponents would come to power, as he himself had dealt most harshly with Sakharam Bapu and others, whose property he had relentlessly confiscated. In fact, Nana suffered the same fate as Sakharam Bapu, at the hands of Baji Rao II. Nana is usually credited with having taken measures for preserving the independence of the Maratha State, but it is difficult to understand how his concentration of all power in his own hands or his large private fortune was going to achieve this result after his death. Why should we assume that Nana was more solicitous about the welfare of the State than Mahadji, who could have easily taken that credit for himself? We often unsuspectingly assume that Nana was the State and that he alone could save it. Let us learn to discard unwarranted assumptions in judging historical questions. Mahadji, on the other hand, did for a time successfully withstand and keep down the British ambitions and would have done greater service if he had lived long enough. So I think Nana would have acquired a much higher place in history, had he subordinated his love of power and monetary interest to the service of the nation, by allowing a chance to others for managing the affairs of the State. Nana and Mahadji had sworn to be brothers and to support each other in all situations, and it must be said to their credit that although they differed often radically, they never allowed matters to proceed to an open rupture between themselves.

LECTURE VII

THE DOWNFALL OF THE MARATHA STATE

1. The Peshwa's regime hastening to its end

For a long time matters were assuming a threatening aspect between the Peshwa's government and the Nizam owing to the latter's failure to pay the large accumulated arrears of tribute. Mahadji was anxious to employ his trained battalions and wipe the Nizam out of existence. The latter had hoped that the British would readily assist him with troops to ward off the danger of an attack from the Marathas. The crisis arose towards the end of 1794 after the death of Mahadji Sindia earlier in that year. Nana Phadnis collected a large Maratha army at Poona and invaded the Nizam's territories. The Nizam also came from the east prepared to oppose the Marathas. The two armies met at Kharda about 150 miles due east of Poona. The Marathas inflicted a crushing defeat and exacted a treaty on paper containing severe terms from the Nizam. The victory was in many senses a crowning glory for the Marathas, as this was the last signal occasion on which most of the prominent Maratha sardars and jagirdars assembled at Poona for a common purpose, offering cordial obedience to the young Peshwa, and giving the outside world an impression that after all the troubles of a generation, the Maratha nation had recovered their former prestige and grandeur. But this was only a passing show. Closely following the victory of Kharda, the promising Peshwa developed the malady of a slow fever, which weakened him so fearfully that he could not stand and yet he could not avoid the tremendous exertions involved in the Dussara celebrations (Oct. 22, 1795). On that day his fever rose very high, and two days afterwards he fell down in a swoon from the balcony of his palace fracturing his thigh, and died in another two days without recovering consciousness. This sad incident dashed the hopes of the nation finally to pieces. After long deliberations and bickerings between Nana Phadnis and the other ministers, the hated Raghoba's son Bajirao II was brought out of confinement at Junnar and invested with the robes of Peshwaship. This sealed the doom of the Marathas. Both in character and capacity Bajirao was utterly worthless and he courted the support of an equally incompetent young lad, Daulatrao Sindia, the successor of Mahadji. The strong battalions of Sindia trained under French officers were of no avail to him as he had not the skill to keep them under proper control. A bitter enmity arose between the Peshwa and the young Holkar, Yashwantrao, who was a spirited and brave but rather impetuous soldier. In order to take revenge upon the Peshwa for the cruel death he had inflicted upon his brother Vithoji, Yashwantrao came upon Poona with a large and devoted army and demanded justice for his grievances which the Peshwa haughtily flouted. In a pitched battle on the outskirts of the city, the Peshwa's army was routed and he ran for life first to Raigad and Mahad and thence by sea to Bassein, where he contracted the famous treaty with Resident Col. Close, agreeing to subsidize British troops to help him to regain his Peshwaship. Thus the independence of the Maratha raj was lost, on the last day of 1802. How in the next year Arthur Wellesley reinstated the Peshwa in his capital, inflicted crushing defeats upon the combined armies of Sindia and the Raja of Nagpur and how Lord Lake in the north won brilliant victories by capturing Delhi and the Emperor from Sindia's custody, are matters of common knowledge and need not be pursued in detail here. British supremacy over India was quickly accomplished and the Maratha supremancy vanished for ever.

2. *Marquess of Hastings on Baijrao II*

The contrast between the two representatives of the Maratha and the British States, Bajirao and the

Marquess of Hastings opposing each other in their final struggle, is indeed most striking. The consummate ability of the latter is apparent in every step he took to compass the Maratha downfall. I cannot resist the temptation of quoting a few lines from his *Private Journal*, which is full of historical interest. Writes the Marquess of Hastings on 23-3-1817 and during the succeeding months : "Towards the close of last year we discovered traces of many intrigues of the Peshwa's, which bore the appearance of hostility to us. It appears that even in the autumn of last year he was soliciting Sindia, Holkar, Ameerkhan, the Gaekwar, the Raja of Nagpur and the Nizam to join with him and drive the English out of India. I shall now rivet such shackles upon Sindia and Holkar as that all the treachery they are at this moment meditating, will be impotent. In fact the downfall of the Marathas is achieved."

For fifteen years the last Peshwa carried on his precious existence and had ultimately to surrender to the force of British arms in his final struggle with them. This period of fifteen years between the Treaty of Bassein in 1802 and the final submission of the Peshwa in 1818, was one of peculiar unrest and uncertainty for all India, owing particularly to the undefined spheres of the various chiefs and potentates, who did not know what to choose between rebellion against and submission to the British power. Historically studied, it is almost a virgin field for investigation. I may mention here in passing that the Alienation Office at Poona possesses a rare collection of old English records, known as the Poona Residency Files, which is a veritable mine of valuable information concerning all Indian States from the Punjab to the south, as it contains profuse despatches penned by prominent British diplomats who ably supported and carried out the measures emanating form the central Government. These files have now been studied and selections are being printed in a series known as the Poona Residency Correspondence." So far eleven volumes have been published.

3. *Bajirao's last effort*

From 1803 to 1818 Bajirao enjoyed a sleepy existence at Poona, under the supervision of a British Resident. While he had no ability to regain his lost position as the head of the Maratha confederacy, he committed the folly of nursing a secret feeling of resentment against the British power and employed all kinds of subterfuges to overcome them. But he received no support from his nation, who deeply resented his acceptance of British aid at Bassein at the sacrifice of liberty. Instead of consolidating his position and conciliating his subordinates, he used British help to put them down. But his hatred towards the British went on increasing and he felt his thraldom so irksome that he waited ardently for a chance to strike a blow against them. Such a chance did indeed occur during the period of the Nepal War (1814-1816). Writes Sir A. Lyall : "The war in Nepal encouraged among the Marathas an inclination to try conclusions again with the English. The Peshwa began to assemble troops and collect military stores. The Pindhari horses became a perpetual menace to the country. They maintained a secret understanding with the Maratha rulers of Poona, Nagpur, Gwalior and Indore. The difficulties and reverses which the British suffered in the Nepal war at its initial stages, inspired the Marathas with some hope of finding their opportunity for re-establishing their lost power." Indeed, had there been a capable leader to organize all the scattered elements of Maratha power and present a united opposition to the British, that moment was certainly auspicious, and the Maratha national sentiment very favourable. But the cool and calculating Marquess of Hastings once more proved a match for any Indian move towards unity. He bided his time quietly while the Nepal War was on, and having effectively closed it in March 1816, he brought the whole weight of the British power to bear against any Indians who dared to defy it, with the result that all traces of opposition in India were finally extinguished in less than a year.

4. *Causes of the Maratha downfall*

During my previous discourses I have now and then explained what the strong and weak points of the Maratha character are, from which one can easily conclude, why they failed to build up a permanent national Government either for the whole of India or even for the Maratha portion of it.

The foregoing discourse coupled with the briefer remarks now and then thrown in, must, I hope, have made it amply clear in what exact direction one could look for the real and immediately relevant causes of the Maratha downfall. In the investigation of this subject we must become very precise. It is no use pointing out the merely general causes, for there is no phenomenon in this mortal world for which many general circumstances and situations cannot be assigned as causes. What history needs is the particular circumstances or conditions which could directly produce the results we are called upon to explain. Later on I am going to deal even with the general causes which many writers of eminence have in their own way put forth. It should also be remembered in this connection that many scholars who have dealt with the subject have alluded to it incidentally and in a manner suited to the line of argument they were following. Some have unconsciously treated the subject with a view to suit their preconceived notions. Such at any rate, is my impression of their treatment, wherever my own views differ from theirs.

I can unhesitatingly attribute the Maratha downfall primarily to the incapacity of the two frivolous youths, Peshwa Bajirao II. and Daulatrao Sindia who, owing to a fortuitous coincidence, came into possession of supreme power in the Maratha State. Their misdeeds brought the Poona court and society to such a moral degradation that no one's life, property or honour was safe. People even in distant parts of the land had to suffer terrible misery through misrule, oppression, plunder and devastation. The sardars and jagirdars, particularly of the Southern

Maratha Country, were so completely alienated that they rushed for escape into the arms of the English. If two such individuals as Bajirao and Daulatro, it may be argued, could wantonly wreck the solid structure of generations, it certainly presupposes a want of proper organization or an accepted constitution for the State. This is doubtless true. If we were an organized government, even these two incapable youths could have been set aside to make room for a more competent agency. But it must even then be conceded that in all human affairs one individual alone can often do or undo any good or great work. Just as one Shivaji could build the Maratha raj, so could one Bajirao destroy it. Individuals mar history as much as they make it. The want of a competent organizer at the head of the State at a critical period, as Munro has emphatically asserted, is the first prominent cause of ruin. While Bajirao and Daulatrao were playing their wicked game, thoughtful men were not wanting who felt a strong impulse to come forth and improve matters, but the two youths proved too powerful for such weak and scattered reforming forces. These latter could have gained strength and asserted themselves, had there been no capable British rivals on the opposite side to turn to the best advantage the least drawback or loop-hole on the Maratha side. Yashwantrao Holkar tried his best to remove Bajirao and put in his place his brother Amritrao, and Arthur Wellesley has remarked that if Amritrao had been the Peshwa, there would have been no chance for the British to establish their supremacy. But such a consummation was purposely prevented by them through skilful diplomatic and strategic moves. In fact Bajirao always taunted his British helpers with the remark, "You came as friends and allies to help me retain my power, while you tried your best to pull me down." There is no escape from this dilemma. I shall later on refer to the strong contrast between the personnel of the two Powers confronting each other and to the superior politics and organization of the British, which easily explain the Maratha fall.

5. *Neglect of science*

In addition to the particular causes mentioned above several general ones can also be pointed out. Among these may be mentioned the utter neglect of the study of science and of military training and organization. Those who conducted the State, failed to take note of what their European neighbours —the Portuguese, the French and the British,—were doing in India, and how they maintained their influence. Bajirao I., and his brother Chimnaji conquered Bassein from the Portuguese after a heroic fight of which the nation ever after talked proudly, but failed to take the logical step that the experience of their naval fighting with the Portuguese should have suggested, *viz.*, the foundation of a naval arsenal and a ship building base, as measures of self-defence. The Portuguese had docks, foundries for making guns, and experts to work them on scientific methods. These should have been continued under Indian management at Bassein instead of indenting Portuguese gunners into Maratha employ like Noronha (or Musa Naran as he is known to Marathi readers). If the Portuguese base at Bassein had been kept in order and continued to be worked for naval purposes, the Peshwa would not have been under the necessity of calling for British help fifteen years later to bring the Angrias to obedience.

The Peshwas had numerous occasions to apply to those western nations for a supply of shot, powder and cannon, and often lost their campaigns for want of these materials. The necessary education and equipment could have been easily acquired and Indian experts trained. Contemporary papers make frequent mention of how statues, pictures, swords, English iron and lead, guns, telescopes, files, medicines, clocks, articles of cutlery and crockery, paper and numerous other articles of daily use, used to be constantly obtained, by way of present or purchase from Europe ; and yet it did not occur to any of us to enquire how these articles were manufactured and why they could not be produced here. Printing presses and newspapers were known to exist in Calcutta, Goa and Pondicherry. Western surgery was often resorted to by very many Indians of position and means. Peshwa Madhav Rao I. himself employed a European physician to treat him. There is mention of even gum-plaster being obtained from the British at Bombay , but intelligent and keen as these Peshwas and their advisers were, one certainly fails to understand why they utterly neglected the study and development of science, so essentially needed for the preservation of their independence. We talk glibly of the selflessness and self-sacrifice which, we claim, our religion enjoins on us. But can we show any sacrifice of ours which can even distantly compare with the tremendous sacrifice of life and money, which the western nations have made for centuries past, in the pursuit of science, exploration, in their admirable perseverance, for instance, in developing the aeroplane or exploring the polar regions or climbing the heights of the Himalayas? It is certainly this spirit of science and enquiry, this perseverance and enterprise, this readiness to undergo hardship and privation in an abstract cause, so generally lacking in the East, which is mainly responsible for our downfall. Until we achieve this spirit, all talk of independence or *Swaraj* seems hopeless. How to create this spirit must be the first concern of those who are striving to regenerate India.

6. *Neglect of Artillery*

As early as the commencement of the 16th century, the Portuguese battle-ships successfully employed siege guns in conquering important places like Goa on the west coast. A few years thereafter Babar established his Mughal Empire in India chiefly by means of guns. He borrowed the art of gunnery from the Turks, who had captured Constantinople 75 years before him with the same weapon. The Europeans developed this arm of warfare very rapidly and with its help expanded their trade, power and influence throughout the world, by naval enterprises. But the Marathas or any other Indian power never made this art their own. They got a few men trained by Bussy, mostly Muslims and Christians, to cope with the artillery of Ahmad Shah Abdali in 1760. The Peshwa took up Ibrahim Khan Gardi, and later on Nana Phadnis employed Musa Naran and Mahadji Sindia engaged De Boigne in 1784 and Perron and other French officers a few years later. But why Maratha administrators of the type of Mahadji and Nana Phadnis did not train their own men in this essential branch of warfare, passes our comprehension, except on the supposition that the Marathas feared that it would make them lose religion and caste. To handle machines and engines requires hard, constant labour, neglecting ease and laying aside the injunctions of caste. They tried to preserve religion at the sacrifice of science. They had therefore to depend upon foreigners for a most vital means of self-protection, and since the old Maratha system of guerilla warfare could not stand against organized artillery and trained infantry, it went out of use and there was nothing else to take its place. Shivaji used both systems according to his need. Guerilla warfare came into vogue first with Malik Ambar under whom Shahji learnt it and later practised it with advantage against Shah Jahan. Shahji's son Shivaji developed it into a magnificent weapon of warfare, which proved most useful particularly during the Maratha war with Aurangzeb; Santaji Ghorpade, Dhanaji Jadhav, Khanderao Dabhade, Peshwa Bajirao I, in the earlier days, and the Sindias, the Holkars, and others in later days, being the efficient leaders in that mode of fighting. But when the Karnatak wars between the French and the English exemplified the value of long range guns with regiments of infantry to cover them, the Maratha tactics underwent a rapid change. The Peshwa did establish an artillery department at Poona and other places, under a Brahman sardar named Panse, but the attempt was crude in the absence of proper scientific knowledge; and in addition, they never could get together sufficient Maratha infantry or ensure the training and organization required to bring it into operation at the critical moment.

The first open abandonment of the guerilla method took place at Panipat where the famous Bhau had the greatest confidence in the artillery corps of Ibrahim Khan Gardi. Their failure at Panipat was not due so much to the change of tactics as to other causes into which it is not necessary to go here. But generally after Panipat the old tactics fell gradually into disuse. Mahadji Sindia noticed plainly and carefully the havoc which the British guns and their organized infantry regiments made during the campaign of Talegaum ; he was surprised to see the British regiments standing firm like solid walls. He had also the same experience in Gujarat the next year. No Maratha leader had the courage to face the British guns however few they might be. Mahadji therefore determined to organize his army on the European model as soon as he was free from the entanglement of war with the British. He employed French officers who unfortunately could not be depended upon in critical times. and who proved too much for Daulatrao, the weak successor of Mahadji. At Agra and other places excellent fire-arms used to be manufactured under French direction, but Bajirao II and Daulatrao Sindia did not care to maintain this branch of their fighting strength. Writes Sir Jadunath Sarkar, " When Raymond's Corps was disbanded in 1798, its stores at Hyderabad contained small arms and clothing for 12000 men beyond the force then serving under Mr. Piron, besides a number of pistols for cavalry. The French corps had three arsenals and two foundries. The arsenal near their lines at Hyderabad was full of military stores, and in the foundry there were a number of brass cannon newly cast, which the English Artillery officers judged as good and as well-finished as any they had ever seen. They also made swords, muskets and pistols. The French party were always well paid ; their clothing was neat and their discipline superior to those in a native service. "* Had the central Maratha Government possessed the necessary foresight and perseverance to organize their fighting

---

**Islamic culture*, Jan. 1933.

and directing machine, it appears plain that they would have been able to resist the British advance successfully. But this presupposes an organized system of government of which I shall now speak.

7. *Lack of organization.*

Another potent cause of our downfall has been our utter lack of organization or system in anything that we undertake, whether a government office or a department, or a campaign against an enemy. There is as a rule no unity of command, no distribution of work and power, no clear-cut assignment of duties, no method, no system, no rule. This has particularly been the case with the Marathas, who by nature are not amenable to discipline or inclined to any concerted action, each one pulling independently. This has been a national weakness which was only kept in check for a time by outstanding personalities like Shivaji, Baji Rao I. or Madhav Rao I. Want of precise attention to details and pre-arrangement has been the constant drawback of all Indians. If we examine minutely why the Rajputs failed again and again against, say, Mahmud of Ghazni or Muhammad Ghori, or why Alauddin Khilji or Babar or Akbar scattered large Hindu armies at a stroke, we shall notice this prominent defect throughout, that is, there never was a perfect unity of command or a clear division and co-ordination of work on the side of the Hindus. Several Rajput princes assembled to fight the common enemy, each one coveting the honour but not the risk, of taking the supreme command. Ahmad Shah Abdali's circumspection at Panipat deserves to be remembered in this connection. Whenever there were proposals for negotiating peace with the Marathas or interference with the fighting arrangements, Ahmad Shah always reminded his allies, as Kashirai puts it lucidly, " I am not a diplomat, I am only a soldier. So leave the business of fighting entirely to me and you may carry on your business of negotiation as you please." Whenever the Marathas have lost, it will invariably be found that the failure was due to want of proper organization and a divided command. The Maratha system of Government and their division of spheres among the various jagirdars were mainly responsible for this cardinal defect, *viz.*, their centrifugal tendency, of which I have spoken before. Unity of command presupposes pre-eminent qualities in a commander. He must be able to enforce rigid discipline upon all whom he has to lead. The Maratha jagirdars became entirely disorganized when power fell into the incompetent hands of Baji Rao II. Every one saw the necessity of uniting for a common purpose, but tried to save his own skin at the sacrifice of others, so that when in the second Maratha War, Sindia and the Raja of Nagpur called upon Yashvant Rao Holkar to come and join them against the British, Yashvant Rao remained studiously aloof, waiting for the outcome of the war the other two were fighting, and when the British, after smashing the power of Sindia and the Raja of Nagpur directed their arms against Yashvant Rao, his eyes were at last opened and he piteously wrote letters to all other Marathas to come and join him. The letter that he wrote is typical and will bear reproduction here : " We have all heretofore united to defend our Hindu empire ; but recently, owing to family dissensions, our empire and our religion have both been declining. Their final ruin cannot be prevented unless we all unite and work together. I am doing all I can to achieve this object and am sworn to pursue it to the end of my life. I call upon God to help me. But it is no use doing this single-handed, and all of you remaining mere idle spectators, each one looking to his personal interest. It behoves you all to combine for the defence of our empire and religion. " But this appeal which he himself had disregarded the year before, now came too late and could not mend matters.

8. *The Maratha and the British personnel,—a contrast*

History has often to take account of fortuitous circumstances which are usually beyond the power of human reason to account for. Similarly I cannot pass over what is usually called an unforeseen conjunction in the affairs of the Maratha kingdom. At any rate, since the downfall of the Marathas is synchronous with the end of the 18th and the beginning of the 19th centuries, the contrast in the relative personnel of the Marathas and the British becomes all the more striking. While one can admit that the Marathas were much inferior to the British in point of organization, and proficiency in science and arms, we must also remember that the Marathas were by no means inferior, but much superior, to any other Indian power or State of that time. The element of chance lies only in this, that before the Marathas had time to improve the scattered position of the jagirdars and consolidate their strength under a clever administrator, they were called upon to oppose the formidable British power strong in science, constitution, unity, and naval supremacy. Between 1794 and 1800 most of the experienced and able persons in the Maratha kingdom were removed by the cruel hand of death. The old Ramshastri had already passed away on 11th November 1789. Mahadji Sindia died on 12th February 1794, being followed by Haripant Phadke four months later (on 19th June 1794), and by Ahalyabai Holkar a year later (on 13th August, 1795). The young Peshwa Madhav Rao, who since his birth had been the joy and hope of the nation, lost his life on 27th October 1795 by an accidental fall from the balcony of his palace. The subsequent deaths of Tukoji Holkar on 15th August 1797 and of Parshuram Bhau Patwardhan on 18th September 1799 and last of all, that of Nana Phadnis on 13th March 1800, closed the final chapter of the Maratha Swaraj founded by Shivaji.

Just at the time that death played this havoc, the supreme power fell into the hands of an incapable and unscrupulous and intensely selfish Peshwa, Baji Rao II., who was quite unequal to the task which he was called upon to perform. He never trusted those who had been brought up under the old regime but selected his advisers from worthless menials, selfish priests, or intriguing upstarts like Sarjerao Ghatge, of whose misdeeds the less said the better. How could a worthless profligate like

12

Bajirao, surrounded by men of small minds and poor character, hold his own against a phalanx of eminent personalities, on the side of the British, the masters of their age ? Lord Wellesley the Governor General and his two brothers Arthur and Henry Wellesley, were men of extraordinary capacity and talent. Arthur Wellesley (afterwards Duke of Wellington) was destined to be the conqueror of Napoleon. Mountstuart Elphinstone, Sir John Malcolm, Sir Barry Close, Col. Collins, Jonathan Duncan, and a little later Sir Thomas Munro, have all left behind them unequalled reputations even if we do not mention Jenkins, Lake and many others, second only to these. The nation which possesses such able personalities for its agents is bound to win success at any time. Why the junction of the two centuries should be marked by such a terrible contrast in the politics of India, is difficult to explain, except by attributing it to chance, which our great philosophy of the *Bhagwad Gita* emphatically admits as the fifth cause of every human affair !* The Marathas had tided over several severe crisis in their career. The great Shivaji was followed by an incompetent son who nearly lost the kingdom ; the death of Aurangzeb brought on another crisis, that of a civil war. Tara Bai's foolish ambition unnecessarily added to the troubles brought on by the death of Shahu. Even the battle of Panipat was not devoid of this element of chance. The untimely death of Peshwa Madhav Rao I. created the last great crisis which nearly disjointed the whole Maratha political fabric. The long history of England also is not without this element of chance, producing crisis at different periods of its existence. After all, history is a justification of Providence.

9. *False notion of religion*

But why we failed to keep pace with the scientific progress so essential for the existence of a nation any-

---

*अधिष्ठानं तथा कर्ता करणं च पृथग्विधम् ।
विविधाश्च पृथक् चेष्टा दैवं चैवात्र पंचमम् ॥

where and at any time, is also an interesting point for us to investigate. We Hindus have great achievements to our credit in the past. Art and science did exist and progress in India up to a certain time, as the architecture of the Hindu and Muslim periods, our finest textiles, our arts and literatures, our advance in mathematics and astronomy, our ancient sea-borne trade, and various other achievements of a like nature, were not possible without a proper spirit of study and enquiry. When and how we lost this spirit is a point worth considering. I think towards the end of the 13th century, *viz.*, about the days of Ramdeorao Yadav and his great minister Hemadri, the attention of our society in general was for the first time diverted to a false notion of religious merit, *i.e.*, to pursuits of a superstitious nature, making caste restrictions rigid, enjoining upon us various religious practices as the only means of happiness and salvation, and introducing thousands of minute rules and practices entirely antagonistic to the material interests of a progressive community. Alauddin Khilji was the first Muhammadan who crossed the Narmada into the south and put an end to the independence of the Yadavas of Devagiri at the beginning of the 14th century, which I take to be a great landmark in Indian history, when the old order of society and politics markedly changed, making room for innovations of an undesirable character.

Hemadri, the great minister of the Yadav kings, was a learned pandit and patron of Sanskrit learning, and used his great influence, scholarship and energy in bringing about what I may call an entire revolution in society and religion. He employed a large number of pandits for several years and compiled with their help out of old *shastras* and existing practices, his great work called *Chaturvarga Chintamani*, a comprehensive compilation in four parts, *viz.*, 1st *Vrata-Khanda* (religious vows to different deities). 2nd *Dana-Khanda* (charities to Brahman priests), 3rd *Tirtha-Khanda* (pilgrimage to holy places) and 4th *Moksha-khanda* (the attainment of salvation). These practically covered the whole life of a Hindu. Being an intensely practical man, Hemadri revolutionized very many arts of life also. He is the author of a style of building houses and temples, which till recently was universal in Maharastra, and of a style of cursive writing of the Devanagari characters now known as *Modi*. If we examine this great compilation of Hemadri, we shall find that he has prescribed in all some 2,000 practices or vows, repetitions, incantations for driving away evil spirits, rites and ceremonies, penances and punishments, prayers and cures, charities and offerings of various kinds, which it is needless to mention here. So that, if every member of society were to practise them all, he would have to do at least five or seven of them each day through the year. The various deities are mentioned with details as to how they should be propitiated, what articles of diet were liked by each, how Brahmans should be fed at the worship of each deity, all purporting to occupy men's time and energy for the attainment of religious merit and the salvation of the soul, leaving no room for the ordinary concerns of life and making the people perfectly oblivious of the fact that they had any secular duties to perform. Even travel to foreign countries was prohibited.

During some 300 years after Hemadri the influence of this compilation continued to divert men's minds from study and progress; indeed, the traces of that system are to be found even in our own day. Since the 14th century two main ideals of life have influenced men's minds in India,—the one that of the religious practices just mentioned, which I have termed the School of Hemadri, although many other authors of great learning and note in other provinces also worked in the same direction, such as Shulapani Upadhyaya and Raghunandan Bhattacharya, as also the great lawyers of the Bhatta family of Benares, viz., Narayan Bhatta, Kamalakar Bhatta and Nilkantha. All these laid down, as I said, one ideal of life, which was picked up mostly by the upper classes of the priestly persuasion. The other ideal which was mainly accepted by the lower classes or the ignorant masses, was represented by saints like Kabir, Nanak, Eknath and Chaitanya, whose theme was the spread of the *Bhagavata Dharma* or the *Bhakti* cult, *i.e.*, devotion and prayers. Their object was to translate all religious thought from Sanskrit into the vernaculars and create equality and universal brotherhood among all classes of the people, enjoining upon them humble and sincere devotion to God as the only means of salvation. Both the ideals turned men's thoughts away from any original study of the physical sciences. In my opinion, our dark ages commenced just about the time when they ended in Europe.

Ranade has described a movement for religious revival in Europe also, at the same time as in India, but there it was a thorough change from the old to the new, as we know from the lives of men like Luther and Bacon. In Europe, the religious reform followed the Renaissance and did not prevent attention to science and progress. A hundred years before Shivaji, Sir Thomas More laid down fresh lines of progress and education in England. A few years before More, Columbus and others, with the help of mathematics and geography, had made many new discoveries and undertaken voyages throughout the world. The art of printing had commenced to diffuse knowledge and enfranchise men's minds from superstition. The average education in Europe was then far superior to and of a more practical nature than that which was current in India. A list of the Shastris and Pandits of Shivaji's days has been published in one of the volumes printed by the *Bharat Itihas Mandal* of Poona, but it contains no name which can compare in depth of knowledge and practical utility, with Bacon or any other European scholar of those days. The list has doubtless many eminent names : but they are all of the old scholastic type, hardly going beyond wordy grammar and logic of the *ghata-pata* kind. Education in Europe liberalized thought and life, made the people bold, active and venturesome, while in India under the two ideals mentioned above, the people remained steeped in ignorance and superstition, self-contented and resigned, seeking salvation in the world beyond, without caring to improve the one they were living in.

10. *Superior British policy.*

The inquisitive nature of the British people and their superior diplomacy added immensely to their strength in comparison with the Marathas. During the first Maratha War the British had full and detailed information in their possession as regards the Maratha Raj, its armies, the comparative worth of the various jagirdars, their mutual relations and their family disputes. The British knew very well who were likely to succumb to outside influences and who were staunchly loyal to the Peshwas. When they commenced the war, they were prepared for any eventuality. Apart from Hornby, Hastings, Mostyn, Anderson, Upton, Malet, Goddard and a few others who were helping directly in the war, there were many other accredited British agents, touring in the country for purposes of trade, and simultaneously obtaining all kinds of information, say, about the Maratha forts and their positions, the paths leading to them, the condition of the people, local disputes and political happenings. This shows how inquisitive the British people are and how carefully they study and collect all useful information and immediately despatch it to the proper authorities. Mostyn was present in Poona at the time of Peshwa Narayan Rao's death, and for seven years supplied useful information to Bombay, Calcutta and Madras in his despatches. In fact, Mostyn may be said to have been the the prime agent who provoked that aggressive war. On the other hand, the Maratha party had hardly any information about the doings of the British people. They knew nothing about England, about the British form of Government, about their settlements and factories in India and outside, their character and inclinations, their arms and armaments ; perhaps even Nana Phadnis did not at all possess such details, so that, while the British were well posted in all matters, the Marathas were woefully ignorant.

There is no example of a Hindu having learnt English during the Maratha regime so as to talk and correspond freely in that language and obtain correct information of the British plans, their intentions and movements, while there was a large number of Englishmen who learnt Indian languages and freely spoke them. An English officer in Wellesley's days delivered an extempore speech in Marathi at Calcutta, which shows the inherent inferiority of the Marathas and accounts for much of their failure as rulers. Even Nana Phadnis was ignorant not only of the geography of the outside world, but even of India. The maps which he used in those days are extant and are fantastic, inaccurate and useless. The art of printing had long been introduced into India by the missionaries. The first English newspaper was started at Calcutta in the early eighties of the 18th century; and the earliest Indian vernacular types and printed books were those of the Christian missions in the late 18th century. As regards travel, the only mention we find of Indians having gone to Europe in the 18th century is that of the agents of Raghoba,—Maniar Parsee and a Hindu named Hanumant Rao who were sent by him about the year 1780 to England in order to obtain British help against the ministerial party at Poona. A letter written by Edmund Burke to Raghoba in the year 1782 exists, in which the Hindu Hanumant Rao is mentioned as almost dying owing to the severe hardships which his religion subjected him to, in the most inclement weather of Britain. Raja Ram Mohan Ray was perhaps the first Hindu of note to visit Europe from India, which he did in 1830 when steamships had come into use while the British had been roaming over the whole world for 300 years before Ram Mohan Ray's time. Indeed, if we take into consideration the tremendous sacrifice of life and money that the British people have made for three centuries during a time when travelling by sea was most dangerous, the prize of world supremacy which they have obtained appears not at all undeserved. The Marathas failed grievously in this point also.

11. How far is caste responsible for our downfall? Peculiar position of the British.

Many writers, Indian and foreign, have put down caste jealousies and social prejudices as a direct cause of the

Maratha downfall. Their reasoning is so vague that it cannot be convincing to every reader, as it is not supported by definite facts and figures. India has doubtless been a caste-ridden country and certainly suffered in various ways owing to this evil, as I have amply shown above. But beyond that religious factor, I have not been able to understand how caste has directly and particularly affected the Marathas. Whatever may be the disadvantages of caste in general, I am of opinion that in this respect we are apt to judge of those times from our experience of present day conditions. Caste did not disable the Marathas from building up a powerful and independent kingdom and hold it by force of arms and policy for nearly 150 years. Indeed wise and eminent personalities like Shivaji or Madhav Rao never allowed caste to interfere with their justice and fair play. A letter is extant in which the prevailing sentiment seems to have been unmistakably expressed in these words : " A government is run by all kinds of people, great and small, good and bad ; but there should be no distinction made on account of their caste. All are equal children of the State ; he who serves the State well should be promoted ; all should be treated with equal attention and kindness. Those who harm the State should be punished, without distinction of caste. Then and then only will the administration go on without disturbance. We, as obedient and loyal servants, know only this, that all castes, whether Deshasthas, Kokanasthas, Karhadas, Prabhus, Shenvis or Marathas, all belong equally to the State and all have an equal claim on the head of the State as their father. Their service alone should be a measure of their worth and not their caste. "*

On the whole, I am not prepared to accuse the earlier Peshwas indiscriminately of showing any undue predilection for the Brahmans. If we make a correct computation, we shall find that during the rule of the Peshwas, 75% of the families that attained prominence then were not certainly non-Brahmans. It is doubtless true that a very large number of Brahman families rose to prominence

---

* ऐतिहासिक पत्रव्यवहार ले. १०० च्या शेवटीं.

particularly during the latter part of the Peshwas' regime, just as many Maratha families rose to distinction in States presided over by Maratha jagirdars. But this is merely human nature. If I have power in hand and have to employ a person for the execution of a certain job, I would naturally select one whom I know personally and in whom I can trust. Unless instances are forthcoming of unworthy Brahmans being given jobs in supersession of worthy candidates of other castes, the mere employment of a certain caste should not form a ground for condemnation. I have noticed no instance of the Peshwas having deliberately put down persons of other castes in order to promote their own, except perhaps during the days of the last Peshwa whose only concern was the propitiation of Brahmans and attainment of religious merit as the best means of serving his raj. Shivaji sternly put down some great Maratha families, Moreys, Mohites, and Ghorpades, and raised Prabhus and Brahmans to power and influence. He paid the highest respect to Ramdas and other worthy Brahmans. Can we detect any caste prejudice in this? It is worth noting that out of the 49 persons found guilty in the murder of Narayan Rao, 24 were Deccani Brahmans of the murdered Peshwa's caste, 2 Saraswats, 3 Prabhus, 6 Marathas, 1 Maratha maid servant, 5 Musalmans and 8 northern Hindus. This analysis will show that caste did not play, so far as the administration went, any significant part.

It is well known how faithfully Ibrahim Khan Gardi served Bhau Saheb on the field of Panipat, against his co-religionist Ahmad Shah Abdali. Muhammad Yusuf, a Gardi leader, who murdered Narayan Rao, was captured for the Peshwas by one Taj Khan Rohilla. How Shivaji's life was saved at Agra by a Musalman *Faras* I have mentioned elsewhere. If some Maratha families of Shivaji's time lost their importance during succeeding days, it was not due to the Peshwas deliberately putting them down. Many Brahman families of Shivaji's time also suffered equally—the Pingles, the Hanumantes, the Amatyas, the Sachivs, the Pratinidhis and a host of others, all more or less lagged behind as soon as the successors of those families ceased to possess personal worth.

In fact, the Maratha regime was particularly welcome as affording plenty of field for all and every person in the land, to show one's worth, whatever caste or rank in society one might have belonged to. This was the great practical benefit all people received from their Swaraj in those days. People got equal opportunity for service and distinction, as the accounts of over 100 different families which I have given in my Marathi books with all available minute details will easily prove. Personal jealousies and mutual bickerings there always were, and will ever remain; but they were not based on the principle of caste. The Sindias and the Holkars have always in history been hostile to each other from generation to generation, which cannot be attributed to caste at all. It is said that during Madhav Rao and Narayan Rao's regime, the Deshasthas and the Kokanasthas were at logger-heads, but this does not stand a critical examination. I can show members of both the castes ranging themselves strongly on each of the opposite sides. For three generations the Peshwas and the families of the Prabhu Chitnises were on the best and most intimate terms; so much so that to a great extent it is the Prabhu Chitnises who helped materially the rise of the Peshwas to eminence.

The greatest strength of the raj at the time of Shivaji and later, lay in this happy co-operation of all castes. When Damaji Gaikwad invaded Poona and Satara in the absence of the Peshwa far away in the east, it was a Maratha and a Prabhu general who saved the position for the Peshwa. If Tara Bai disliked Peshwa Balajirao, she had many Brahmans in her confidence and held in dislike many Marathas also. If Sakharam Hari, a Prabhu, was a staunch supporter of the Kokanastha Raghoba, Abaji Mahadev Sohoni, a Kokanastha and Manaji Phakde, a Maratha, were also his strong supporters.

During the first Maratha War nearly all the Maratha and other generals supported the national cause with great devotion and loyalty to the young Peshwa. Again and again on the battlefields of the Karnatak and the north, at Panipat, at Talegaum, before the forts of Gwalior and Dohad, at Lalsot and Kharda, all castes fought with equal courage and valour under the common banner of the Peshwas and were often led by a Brahman general. Malharrao Holkar was a shepherd by caste but never showed disrespect to Baji Rao I or his sons, on the ground of their being Brahmans. It was customary to hold a dinner at Poona on the anniversary of the death of Baji Rao I., when Sindia, Holkar and other intimate associates of Baji Rao used to be invited, and the principal lady of the Peshwa's house had to serve all the guests at the same time. Once it happened that Malharrao Holkar had his dogs with him when he came to the dinner. Gopika Bai, the lady serving the guests, asked Malharrao not to bring the dogs into the dining room. He replied he would not eat without his dogs sharing his dinner with him, and would rather dine in the outer verandah with his dogs, than come inside near the Brahmans and pollute them. He did not feel at all offended for thus being kept outside. People in Maratha days observed caste distinctions in matters of religious concern only, without letting their working life be affected by them. The objection to inter-caste dinners and the fears of pollution by touch, have been recently accentuated when one caste is said to be above another and unwarranted annoyance is caused thereby. The superiority and inferiority of caste affected in those days purely religious functions, and not the common affairs of life. That is how I look at the question.

But this argument of caste and social barriers requires to be examined from another point of view. Domestic quarrels and caste differences have become stock arguments with very many writers, but there is hardly a fallen nation on the earth whose history is available, in whose case the same causes could not be said to have operated, for human nature being the same all the world over, man's selfishness always tries to profit at the sacrifice of others. In the case of India, at any rate, we have been hearing these same causes repeated again and again since the defeat of Paurav by Alexander the Great, right up to the fall of the Peshwas or even up to the present moment of communal tension. These stock arguments are easy to produce but difficult to refute. Human activity always needs some field of action for profitable enterprise, and so long as the custodians of a nation's interests are able to supply an aim to or opportunities for work to its members, their restless activity will find vent outside and not have occasion to encroach on domestic fields. The greatness of a national leader can therefore be measured by the prospective enterprises which he can place before his followers. Much of a nation's success or failure depends, in my opinion, upon constructive genius and far-sighted stewardship on the part of its leaders. On close examination Shivaji would be found to have temporarily changed the whole genius of the Maratha nation. The system of the British constitution of England has been successful for centuries, because it ensures a succession of capable leaders, who serve the best interests of the nation

A close study of the plentiful papers printed by Forrest and in the volumes of the *Persian Calendars*, shows how cautiously and insidiously the British were slowly undermining the edifice not only of the Maratha State, but of those of the various other Indian potentates as well. Professional traders as the British were, and alien both in religion and nationality, with always a strong basic support from England, they could easily afford to pose as disinterested arbitrators in the numerous internal disputes that necessarily cropped up, upon the dissolution of the central Mughal power. If they succeeded in any hazardous enterprise, as in the case of Plassey, well and good ; if they failed they stood to lose almost nothing ; they could quietly wait for a better opportunity for aggrandizement, as actually happened in the first Maratha War. The several Maratha leaders had till then a common aim and a common field for their ambition and enterprise, which were exemplified on the memorable battlefields of Panipat and Kharda, where all castes and people joined without any social jealousy. I am therefore at a loss to understand how caste could be instrumental in bringing down the Maratha power. It is the fashion of the victors to saddle a fallen nation with all conceivable blemishes, but we, as belonging to it, must not swallow all that we are told or taught, unless our reason is prepared to accept it on evidence.

12. *Prominent Maratha personalities.*

Students must observe the Maratha character as revealed in the various types which they meet with in the course of their reading. The Marathas produced rulers and statesmen, soldiers and generals, judges and financiers, poets and writers, among whom not a few women also have distinguished themselves. They fought and conquered, and often suffered terrible reverses which they bore coolly and patiently. Their careers have not been stained by black deeds of cruelty or treachery. They treated opponents like true warriors with consideration and respect. Chanda Saheb, the Nawab of Arcot, was treated with dignity during his eight years' confinement at Satara. Two Englishmen who remained as hostages with Mahadji Sindia, spoke highly of that nobleman's treatment of them. Mushir-ul-Mulk, the Nizam's minister, was likewise honourably treated when he was a prisoner at Poona. Indeed, some of their troubles arose owing to misplaced clemency, as in the case of Raghunath Rao and Manaji Phakde ; the British in such cases would have done short work of them, as they dealt with Hari Bhide in 1775 whom they blew away from the mouth of a cannon, for an unproved act of treason, while four months later Ganesh Vithal Waghmare was merely confined for a similar offence by Haripant Phadke.

To understand the deeds of Maratha valour and sacrifice, a mere glance at the genealogies of some of the historical families will be enough, *e.g.*, the Sindias or the Patwardhans. The historic and revered Kayastha family of the Chitnises of Satara produced able writers and diplomats for seven consecutive generations, a unique fact in history, and have acquired an imperishable name by their voluminous *bakhars* and other writings. Even if we exclude Shivaji and his *guru* Ramdas, we can find in Maratha history such brilliant names in various professions as Santaji Ghorpade and Dhanaji Jadhav, Ramchandra Nilkantha Amatya and Parashuram Trimbak, Raghuji Bhosle and Trimbakrao Dabhade, Baji Rao, Chimnaji Appa, and Madhav Rao Peshwas, Damaji Gaikwad and Sadashiv Rao Bhau, Ramchandra Baba and Khando Ballal, Mahadji Sindia and Nana Phadnis, Sakharam Bapu and Rama Shastri, Jija Bai. Radhabai Peshwa, Umabai Dabhade, Ahalya Bai, Lakshmi Bai of Jhansi, and very many others, who have illumined Maratha history with unforgettable achievements and cleverly handled all the varied concerns of a nation in power. For the most part they dealt moderately with outsiders and gave India inspiration and hope, driving away the gloom which had overcome all, by supplying, as it were, a practical lesson that even mighty kings could with success be resisted in their evil actions. Thus, the example of the great Shivaji, if it cannot supply us with an ideal, should at least set us a limit, behind which we must not go, but beyond which we may certainly try to aspire.

13. *Munro's reflections on the Maratha strength.*

Even before the last Maratha war was started, Sir Thomas Munro had clearly pointed out some of the principal defects existing among the Marathas. On 12th August 1817 he thus wrote to the Governor General.

" When I consider the weakness of the native States and the character of the chiefs under whose sway they now are, I see little chance of a protracted resistance from them. They have not force to turn our armies and lengthen out the contest by a predatory invasion of our territories. They may run ahead for a few days but will have no time to rest or plunder. They will be exhausted and overtaken. It is not that they want resources, that they have not men and horses, but that there is no one amongst them possessed of those superior talents which are necessary to direct them to advantage.

" There is so little system or subordination in native governments that much more energy is required under them than under the more regular governments of Europe, to give full effect to their resources. Daulatrao Sindia was never formidable even in the height of his power. The great means which he possessed were lost in his feeble hands. The exertions of Holkar against Lord Lake were still weaker than those of Sindia. The power of Holkar's as well as Sindia's government has so much declined since that time (1805), that it is scarcely credible they would venture to oppose us. The superiority of our Government is so great that the event of any struggle is no longer doubtful."

14. *Lingering memory of the past.*

Maratha supremacy indeed came to an end with the Treaty of Bassein in 1802. The few Maratha States* that now exist on sufferance, namely those in Malwa, Gujarat and the Deccan, only serve to put us in mind of our former greatness. When Peshwa Bajirao II. was goaded into a war with the British, the first impulse of the latter was to restore the Maratha Kingdom to its former master the Chhatrapati of Satara. But Lord Hastings decided to destroy finally all rivals who were likely in future to contest British supremacy and with that view created a small subordinate principality at Satara under Pratapsinh who, however, did not enjoy his position long. After twenty years of precarious existence he was accused of conspiring against the British power and was exiled to Benares, where he ended his life in impotent and unrepentant anger. His brother Shahji succeeded him, but as he too died in 1848 without leaving a son behind, the Satara raj was finally annexed by Lord Dalhousie together with another large Maratha State, *viz.*, that of Nagpur, which similarly succumbed to the annexation policy of the same politician in 1854. The small state of Kolaba on the west coast held by a descendant of the once terrible Kanhoji Angre, also became extinct for want of an heir in 1840. The Maratha principality of Tanjore in the extreme south suffered a similar fate

*These have now been merged with free India.

in 1855 with the death of its last Raja Shivaji. The feeling of rancour generated in the Maratha mind by such annexations was exhibited by a few members of that race, such as the Rani of Jhansi, Nanasahib of Bithur and his lieutenant Tatya Tope, who, in their own way, seized the chance offered by the troubles of 1857 and suffered for their rashness, leaving behind them a sad memory of the last faint effort for the resuscitation of the Maratha power. One might in a certain sense even now detect a lingering memory of the same in the average Maratha mind, exhibited in some of the thoughtful writings and utterances in Maharastra during the last fifty years. Let us hope England and India will both shape their future history in mutual agreement.

15. *The task before Indian historians.*

Let us clearly grasp the task before us. Some eminent scholars in Madras have been assiduously tapping the Sanskrit and Tamil sources ; what the people of Maharastra are doing I have already mentioned. I must say that the field of work in regard to Gujarat, Rajputana and other parts of northern India is yet comparatively unexplored. Huge masses of Persian materials, as my friend Sir Jadunath Sarkar has frequently assured me, lie scattered all over this part of the country ; they still await patient and selfless labour from many scholars. What we are doing at present mainly concerns political transactions ; the social and economic spheres have hardly yet been touched. In these days of rapid advancement all round, India can no longer afford to remain isolated from the rest of the world. Careful investigation will tell us many new things which were unknown before. In the latter half of the 18th century we meet with very many personalities in northern India, whom our accepted history condemns. Our own reason must prove or disprove this condemnation. The Emperor Shah Alam II. and his various officers like Mirza Najaf Khan, Mir Jafar, Mir Kasim, Aliwardi Khan, Muhammad Reza Khan, the younger Ghaziuddin (for a time the king-maker of Delhi) the Rohilla Najib Khan and his son Zabeta Khan, Shuja-ud-Daula and his successors, Raja Chait Sinh of Benares, besides various Rajput kings, as also Jat and Sikh leaders, —all these and a host of others, Hindu and Muhammadan, seem to have proved powerless to save the liberty of India. How is it that all wisdom seems suddenly to have departed from this country to the west? May we not suspect that their careers have not yet been examined from our own records and from the Indian point of view? If we search for fresh materials we might perhaps be able to extract from them at least some redeeming features, even in the mistakes and failures of these men. Shall we judge and condemn them without going into all the evidence? Even the lowest criminal is given a chance to defend himself. May not some kindred spirits rise to clear them of the stigma? I appeal for workers and trust they will not be found wanting.

INDEX

[For general topics refer to Maratha, Hindu, Muslim, British etc.]